BROOKINGS INSTITUTION, WASHINGTON, D.C.
INSTITUTE FOR GOVERNMENT RESEARCH

SERVICE MONOGRAPHS
OF THE
UNITED STATES GOVERNMENT
No. 11

THE NATIONAL PARK SERVICE
ITS HISTORY, ACTIVITIES AND ORGANIZATION

AMS PRESS
NEW YORK

THE INSTITUTE FOR GOVERNMENT RESEARCH
Washington, D. C.

The Institute for Government Research is an association of citizens for coöperating with public officials in the scientific study of government with a view to promoting efficiency and economy in its operations and advancing the science of administration. It aims to bring into existence such information and materials as will aid in the formation of public opinion and will assist officials, particularly those of the national government, in their efforts to put the public administration upon a more efficient basis.

To this end, it seeks by the thoroughgoing study and examination of the best administrative practice, public and private, American and foreign, to formulate those principles which lie at the basis of all sound administration, and to determine their proper adaptation to the specific needs of our public administration.

The accomplishment of specific reforms the Institute recognizes to be the task of those who are charged with the responsibility of legislation and administration; but it seeks to assist, by scientific study and research, in laying a solid foundation of information and experience upon which such reforms may be successfully built.

While some of the Institute's studies find application only in the form of practical coöperation with the administrative officers directly concerned, many are of interest to other administrators and of general educational value. The results of such studies the Institute purposes to publish in such form as will insure for them the widest possible utilization.

Officers

Robert S. Brookings, *Chairman*
James F. Curtis, *Secretary*
Frank J. Goodnow, *Vice-Chairman*
Frederick Strauss, *Treasurer*

Trustees

Edwin A. Alderman
Robert S. Brookings
James F. Curtis
R. Fulton Cutting
Frederic A. Delano
Henry S. Dennison
George Eastman
Raymond B. Fosdick
Felix Frankfurter
Edwin F. Gay
Frank J. Goodnow
Jerome D. Greene
Arthur T. Hadley
Herbert C. Hoover
David F. Houston
A. Lawrence Lowell
Samuel Mather
Richard B. Mellon
Charles D. Norton
Martin A. Ryerson
Frederick Strauss
Silas H. Strawn
William H. Taft
Ray Lyman Wilbur
Robert S. Woodward

Director
W. F. Willoughby

Editor
F. W. Powell

INSTITUTE FOR GOVERNMENT RESEARCH

SERVICE MONOGRAPHS
OF THE
UNITED STATES GOVERNMENT
No. 11

THE
NATIONAL PARK SERVICE

ITS HISTORY, ACTIVITIES
AND ORGANIZATION

BY
JENKS CAMERON

D. APPLETON AND COMPANY
NEW YORK   LONDON
1922

Library of Congress Cataloging in Publication Data

Cameron, Jenks, 1879-1957.
　The National Park Service.

　　Original ed. issued as no. 11 of Service monographs of the United States Government.
　　Bibliography: p.
　　1. United States. National Park Service.
　2. National parks and reserves—United States.
I. Series: Brookings Institution, Washington,
D.C. Institute for Government Research.
Service monographs of the United States Government,
no. 11.
SB482.A4C35　　1974　　　　353.008'63　　　72-3024
ISBN 0-404-57111-5

Reprinted, with permission, from a volume in the collections of the Newark Public Library

Reprinted from the edition of 1922, New York and London
First AMS edition published, 1974
Manufactured in the United States of America

International Standard Book Number:
Complete Set: 0-404-57100-X
Volume 11: 0-404-57111-5

AMS Press, Inc.
New York, N.Y. 10003

PUBLICATIONS OF THE
INSTITUTE FOR GOVERNMENT RESEARCH

STUDIES IN ADMINISTRATION

The System of Financial Administration of Great Britain
By W. F. Willoughby, W. W. Willoughby, and S. M. Lindsay

The Budget
By René Stourm
T. Plazinski, Translator; W. F. McCaleb, Editor

The Canadian Budgetary System
By H. G. Villard and W. W. Willoughby

The Problem of a National Budget
By W. F. Willoughby

The Movement for Budgetary Reform in the States
By W. F. Willoughby

Teacher's Pension Systems in the United States
By Paul Studensky

Organized Efforts for the Improvement of Methods of Administration in the United States
By Gustavus A. Weber

The Federal Service: A Study of the System of Personal Administration of the United States Government
By Lewis Mayers

The System of Financial Administration of the United States

PRINCIPLES OF ADMINISTRATION

Principles Governing the Retirement of Public Employees
By Lewis Meriam

Principles of Government Purchasing
By Arthur G. Thomas

Principles of Government Accounting and Reporting
By Francis Oakey, C. P. A.

Principles of Personnel Administration
By Arthur W. Procter

SERVICE MONOGRAPHS OF THE UNITED STATES GOVERNMENT

The Geological Survey
The Reclamation Service
The Bureau of Mines
The Alaskan Engineering Commission
The Tariff Commission
The Federal Board for Vocational Education
The Federal Trade Commission
The Steamboat-Inspection Service
The National Park Service
The Public Health Service
The Weather Bureau
The Employee's Compensation Commission

FOREWORD

The first essential to efficient administration of any enterprise is full knowledge of its present make-up and operation. Without full and complete information before them, as to existing organization, personnel, plant, and methods of operation and control, neither legislators nor administrators can properly perform their functions.

The greater the work, the more varied the activities engaged in, and the more complex the organization employed, and more imperative becomes the necessity that this information shall be available—and available in such a form that it can readily be utilized.

Of all undertakings, none in the United States, and few, if any, in the world, approach in magnitude, complexity, and importance that of the national government of the United States. As President Taft expressed it in his message to Congress of January 17, 1912, in referring to the inquiry being made under his direction into the efficiency and economy of the methods of prosecuting public business, the activities of the national government "are almost as varied as those of the entire business world. The operations of the government affect the interest of every person living within the jurisdiction of the United States. Its organization embraces stations and centers of work located in every city and in many local subdivisions of the country. Its gross expenditures amount to billions annually. Including the personnel of the military and naval establishments, more than half a million persons are required to do the work imposed by law upon the executive branch of the government.

"This vast organization has never been studied in detail as one piece of administrative mechanism. Never have the foundations been laid for a thorough consideration of the relations of all its parts. No comprehensive effort has been made to list its multifarious activities or to group them in such a way as to present a clear picture of what the government is doing. Never has a complete description been given of the agencies through which these activities are performed. At no time has the attempt been made to study all of these activities and agencies with a view to the assignment of each activity to the agency best fitted for its performance, to the avoidance of duplication of plant and work, to the integration of all administrative agencies of the government, so far as may be practicable, into a unified organization for the most effective and economical dispatch of public business."

To lay the basis for such a comprehensive study of the organization and operations of the national government as President Taft outlined, the Institute for Government Research has undertaken the preparation of a series of monographs, of which the present study is one, giving a detailed description of each of the fifty or more distinct services of the government. These studies are being vigorously prosecuted, and it is hoped that all services of the government will be covered in a comparatively brief space of time. Thereafter, revisions of the monographs will be made from time to time as need arises, to the end that they may, as far as practicable, represent current conditions.

These monographs are all prepared according to a uniform plan. They give: first, the history of the establishment and development of the service; second, its functions, described not in general terms, but by detailing its specific activities; third, its organization for the handling of these activities; fourth, the character of its plant; fifth, a compilation of, or reference to, the laws and regulations governing its operations; sixth, financial statements showing its appropriations, expenditures and other data for a period of years; and finally, a full bibliography of the sources of information, official and private, bearing on the service and its operations.

In the preparation of these monographs the Institute has kept steadily in mind the aim to produce documents that will be of direct value and assistance in the administration of public affairs. To executive officials they offer valuable tools of administration. Through them, such officers can, with a minimum of effort, inform themselves regarding the details, not only of their own services, but of others with whose facilities, activities, and methods it is desirable that they should be familiar. Under present conditions services frequently engage in activities in ignorance of the fact that the work projected has already been done, or is in process of execution by other services. Many cases exist where one service could make effective use of the organization, plant or results of other serv-

FOREWORD

ices had they knowledge that such facilities were in existence. With the constant shifting of directing personnel that takes place in the administrative branch of the national government, the existence of means by which incoming officials may thus readily secure information regarding their own and other services is a matter of great importance.

To members of Congress the monographs should prove of no less value. At present these officials are called upon to legislate and appropriate money for services concerning whose needs and real problems they can secure but imperfect information. That the possession by each member of a set of monographs, such as is here projected, prepared according to a uniform plan, will be a great aid to intelligent legislation and appropriation of funds can hardly be questioned.

To the public, finally, these monographs will give that knowledge of the organization and operations of their government which must be had if an enlightened public opinion is to be brought to bear upon the conduct of governmental affairs.

These studies are wholly descriptive in character. No attempt is made in them to subject the conditions described to criticism, nor to indicate features in respect to which changes might with advantage be made. Upon administrators themselves falls responsibility for making or proposing changes which will result in the improvement of methods of administration. The primary aim of outside agencies should be to emphasize this responsibility and facilitate its fulfillment.

While the monographs thus make no direct recommendations for improvement, they cannot fail greatly to stimulate efforts in that direction. Prepared as they are according to a uniform plan, and setting forth as they do the activities, plant, organization, personnel and laws governing the several services of the government, they will automatically, as it were, reveal, for example, the extent to which work in the same field is being performed by different services, and thus furnish the information that is essential to a consideration of the great question of the better distribution and coördination of activities among the several departments, establishments, and bureaus, and the elimination of duplications of plant, organization and work. Through them it will also be possible to subject any particular feature of the administrative work of the government to exhaustive study, to determine, for example, what facilities, in the way of laboratories and other plant and equipment, exist for the prosecution of any line of work and where those facilities are located; or what work is being done in any field of administration or research, such as the promotion, protection and regulation of the maritime interests of the country, the planning and execution of works of an engineering character, or the collection, compilation and publication of statistical data, or what differences of practice prevail in respect to organization, classification, appointment, and promotion of personnel.

To recapitulate, the monographs will serve the double purpose of furnishing an essential tool for efficient legislation, administration and popular control, and of laying the basis for critical and constructive work on the part of those upon whom responsibility for such work primarily rests.

Whenever possible the language of official statements or reports has been employed, and it has not been practicable in all cases to make specific indication of the language so quoted.

CONTENTS

CHAPTER   PAGE

FOREWORD

I. HISTORY   1
- The National Park System a Development of the "National Park Idea" 1
- Distinction Between Parks and Monuments 7
- The Parks and Monuments Prior to 1916 8
- The Movement for the Establishment of the National Park Service 11
- The National Park Service Since 1916 12
- The Several Parks 31
  - Yellowstone 31
  - Yosemite 33
  - Sequoia and General Grant 34
  - Mount Rainier 35
  - Crater Lake 36
  - Wind Cave 36
  - Platt 36
  - Sullys Hill 37
  - Mesa Verde 37
  - Glacier 38
  - Rocky Mountain 39
  - Hawaii 39
  - Lassen 39
  - Mount McKinley 40
  - Grand Canyon 40
  - Lafayette 41
  - Zion 41
  - Hot Springs 42
- The National Monuments 43
- Parks and Monuments Not Administered by the National Park Service 44
- Growth of Popular Interest in the Park System . . . 44

II. ACTIVITIES   50
- Conservation of Physical Features 50
  - Natural Wonders 51
  - Ruins and Historical Structures 51
  - Forests and Plants 52
  - Lakes and Streams 53
- Conservation of Wild Life 53
- Improvement 55
- Maintenance 57
- Protection Service 57
- Publicity 58

xi

CHAPTER	PAGE
III. ORGANIZATION	60
Administration	60
Field Service	61
Editorial Section	62
Law Section	62
Publications Section	63
Individual Park Organization—The Yellowstone	63

APPENDIX

1. Outline of Organization 67
2. Classification of Activities 76
3. Publications 78
4. Laws 80
5. Financial Statements 131
6. Statistics of Visitors 137
7. Bibliography 141
   Index 167

THE NATIONAL PARK SERVICE: ITS HISTORY, ACTIVITIES AND ORGANIZATION

CHAPTER I

HISTORY

The National Park Service is a bureau of the Department of the Interior, being the ninth bureau to be established in that department. It is engaged in the supervision, management, and control of those national parks and monuments which are under that department's jurisdiction. It was created by the act of August 25, 1916 (39 Stat. L., 535), but did not begin to function until after the approval of the deficiency appropriation act of April 17, 1917 (40 Stat. L., 20) which provided funds for its establishment.

The National Park System a Development of the "National Park Idea." Though the National Park Service is of recent origin the system of national parks of which it is an outgrowth dates back half a century to the creation, in 1872, of the Yellowstone National Park, the first true national park established in the United States. Inasmuch as the creation of the Yellowstone was the result of a conception of the conservation of natural wonders which has come to be known as the "National Park Idea," it will be proper at this point to discuss briefly, first the events leading up to the inception of the idea; and, second, its subsequent development.

The existence of the natural wonders which occur in such profusion in the upper Yellowstone country had been known early in the last century to a few wandering hunters and trappers who visited the region in search of beaver. John Colter, a hunter who had accompanied Lewis and Clark on their expedition to the Pacific, visited the park region in 1807, and was probably the first white man to see the curiosities it contained. Lewis and Clark themselves, in 1806, skirted the region, and just missed becoming its discoverers by about fifty miles.

During the heyday of the fur trade a few other trappers found their way into the neighborhood, and in the era of gold-hunting which went on over the entire mountain country after 1849, some prospectors also visited it.

Practically all of these men, from Colter down, brought back accounts, some truthful, some exaggerated, of the wonders they had seen in the shape of geysers, hot springs, etc. These accounts, however, were almost universally disbelieved, Colter's being hailed with especial derision, and the thermal region he described coming to be known popularly as "Colter's Hell."

The persistency of these hunters' tales, however, and their essential agreement resulted eventually in the arousing of curiosity. In Montana especially there developed a desire to settle definitely the truth or falsity of the rumors of amazing phenomena around the upper reaches of the Yellowstone. This resulted, in 1869, in the first expedition which had for its definite object the exploration of the much-talked-of area.

This expedition, consisting of David E. Folsom, C. W. Cook, and William Peterson, spent a month in the park region in September-October, 1869, during which time they investigated a considerable number of the principal phenomena which it contains. Mr. Folsom afterwards wrote an excellent narrative of the party's exploration which was first published in the "Western Monthly" of Chicago, and subsequently (1894) published in pamphlet form by Hon. N. P. Langford, the first superintendent of the Yellowstone Park, who added an interesting preface.

In the following year, Mr. Langford was a member of the

HISTORY 3

second exploring expedition to enter the region, the Washburn-Doane expedition, so-called from its being led by General Henry D. Washburn, Surveyor-General of Montana, and Lieutenant G. C. Doane of the United States Army, who commanded a military escort detailed by the War Department. This expedition spent about a month in the region, but explored it somewhat more thoroughly than the Folsom party had done.

The published reports of these two expeditions aroused intense interest throughout the entire country, and had much to do with the sending out of a government expedition in 1871 under the joint auspices of the Geological Survey and the Engineer Corps of the Army, well equipped for the making of precise scientific observations. This expedition made a large collection of accurate data concerning the entire region and took a great many photographs. From the standpoint of exact information obtained it was the most important of the three expeditions.

For a less ponderable but far more momentous reason, when viewed in the light of its effect upon subsequent events, the Washburn-Doane expedition, nevertheless, must be given first place among these pioneer explorations of the Yellowstone region. It was on this expedition that expression was first given to the thought which has been responsible for the creation and development of the Country's system of national parks. At a camp fire of this expedition, on September 19, 1870, the members were discussing the wonders they had seen and the certainty of the remarkable area becoming a mecca for tourists. This led to the suggestion by several that it would be a "profitable speculation" to take up land surrounding the principal phenomena and exploit them as commercial enterprises. Objection to this point of view was expressed by Cornelius Hedges, a member of the party, to the effect that the recently discovered wonderland should never be allowed to pass into private ownership, but should be set aside for the use and enjoyment of all the people. The other members of the party at once fell in with this higher conception of the matter, and all agreed to unite in an endeavor to make it an accomplished fact. This was the beginning of the "National Park Idea."

So widespread was the popular interest resulting from the publication of articles by various members of the several expeditions; and so vigorously was the project for the erection of the Yellowstone Country into a public park pushed by several leading members of the Washburn-Doane expedition and by Dr. F. V. Hayden of the Geological Survey, one of the leaders of the Government expedition of 1871, that in less than two years after Mr. Hedges made his novel proposition the Act of Dedication creating the Yellowstone National Park, received the signature of President Grant (Act of March 1, 1872; 17 Stat. L., 32.)

The text of this measure will be found in the appendix. Attention will be called at this point to its three outstanding features:

The setting aside of the Yellowstone region "as a public park or pleasuring-ground";

A provision making mandatory "the preservation, from injury or spoliation, of all timber, mineral deposits, natural curiosities, or wonders within said park, and their retention in their natural condition";

A provision making mandatory the protection of the fish and game in the park area against "wanton destruction" or "capture or destruction for the purposes of merchandise or profit."

The law also provides that the Secretary of the Interior shall have exclusive control of the park, and it charges him with the making of rules and regulations necessary for the carrying out of its provisions.

The national park system began with the passage of this law, the large significance of which is well expressed by General Hiram M. Chittenden:

It was, a notable act, not only on account of the transcendent importance of the territory it was designed to protect, but because it was a marked innovation in the traditional policy of governments. From time immemorial privileged classes have been protected by law, in the withdrawal, for their exclusive enjoyment, of immense tracts for forests, parks and game preserves. But never before was a region of such vast extent as the Yellowstone Park set apart for the use of all the people without distinction of rank or wealth.[1]

It is proper, at this point, to make a slight digression in order to make clear a somewhat anomalous situation that has long existed with regard to the question—if it be a question—as to what park of the present national park system was the first to be established. The Yellowstone has been referred to above as the first true national park. As has just been pointed out, its establishment was the direct result of the birth of the national park idea. Nevertheless there is another park of the system, the Hot Springs National Park, which was set aside almost forty years to a day before the creation of the Yellowstone (Act of April 20, 1832; 4 Stat. L., 505) and which is frequently referred to as the first national park.

To refer to it thus is incorrect, although it might be proper to call it the oldest member of the national park system. The confusion has arisen through the fact that at the time of the creation of the Yellowstone the Hot Springs Reservation in Arkansas was being administered by the Secretary of the Interior, not as a national park, because up until that time such a thing as a national park in the sense we understand it to-day was not dreamed of, but merely as a portion of the public domain which for certain reasons had been withdrawn from settlement or sale. Those reasons pertained to the medicinal springs which the area contained. Their curative properties becoming widely known throughout the country, a fear arose that they might pass into private ownership and be privately exploited. To prevent this was the purpose of the Act of 1832. This law merely states that the area containing

[1] Chittenden, The Yellowstone National Park, p. 79.

the springs "shall be reserved for the future disposal of the United States," and makes no mention of the preservation of natural curiosities in their original state, the protection of wild life, the public pleasure-ground feature, or of any of the elements of the national park idea; and as a matter of fact Congress had no such idea in mind when it set the Hot Springs area aside. Reservation to prevent private exploitation was its only thought.

It may be argued that this was precisely the thought back of the setting aside of the Yellowstone. But there was this difference: Hot Springs represented mere reservation, Yellowstone represented reservation plus development toward a particular end,—the working out of the national park idea.

After the Yellowstone was established the two areas were administered together in the office of the Secretary of the Interior. As other parks were established from time to time— fourteen [2] were created between the founding of the Yellowstone and the establishment of the National Park Service in April, 1917—they were grouped for administrative purposes with Yellowstone and Hot Springs, and they came to be spoken of collectively as the National Parks and the Hot Springs Reservation. They continued to be so referred to even after the creation of the National Park Service in 1916, Hot Springs being called a reservation until the passage of the sundry civil appropriation act for 1921, in which a clause was inserted providing that it should thenceforth be known as "Hot Springs National Park" (Act of March 4, 1921; 41 Stat. L., 1407). As a matter of fact, the real status of Hot Springs, until the time at least of the creation of the Yellowstone, was less that of one of the national parks than of one of the national monuments, of which there are at present twenty-four in the national park system, twenty of which had been created prior to the organization of the National Park Service. Detailed reference to the monuments is made below.

[2] Including one park, Casa Grande, which was later given monument status.

HISTORY

To summarize, the Yellowstone was the first national park, and the system of parks and monuments—including Hot Springs—of which it was the beginning was the direct result of the conception of the National Park Idea.

Distinction between Parks and Monuments. The act of June 8, 1906 (34 Stat. L., 225), entitled "An act for the preservation of American antiquities," gave the President discretionary power to set aside by proclamation any lands owned or controlled by the United States containing "historic landmarks, historic or prehistoric structures, and other objects of historic or scientific interest" as "national monuments." Provision was made also for the punishment by fine or imprisonment of persons injuring the monuments, and jurisdiction over the monuments was given to the Secretary of the Interior, the Secretary of Agriculture, or the Secretary of War, depending upon which department had jurisdiction over the areas in which the monuments were severally located.

Section 4 of the act provides that the secretaries of the three departments—Interior, Agriculture, and War—shall make uniform rules and regulations for the purpose of carrying out its provisions. Secretaries Hitchcock, Wilson, and Taft promptly complied by promulgating—Dec. 28, 1906—an appropriate set of rules which are still in effect without change.

The passage of this act was the culmination of an organized movement by a group of archæologists, scientists, and others, to put such safeguards about the unique archæological treasures which the country possesses in the ancient pueblos and cliff dwellings of the Southwest as would prevent their spoliation and ultimate destruction. Their protection by the creation of additional park areas had been found impracticable because a special congressional enactment was necessary in each case, and because Congress was unwilling to create a great number of parks, many of which would be, necessarily, of very limited area. The original idea had been to protect ancient ruins only, but the act was broadened so as to include within its scope other objects of historic or scientific value, natural as well as artificial. The first monument created, as a matter-of-fact, was the Devils Tower, in Wyoming, a natural formation.

Some confusion has arisen as to the difference between parks and monuments. It has been asked, for example, why, of two reserved areas, the basic reasons for the reservation in each case being the preservation of a natural wonder, one should be a park and the other a monument.

The simplest way to answer this question is to say what has been said above in speaking of the setting-aside of Hot Springs. The object of a monument is the preservation from destruction or spoliation of some object of historic, scientific, or other interest. The object of a park is that and something more; namely, the development of the area reserved for its more complete and perfect enjoyment by the people. It might be said that a monument is park raw material, because many of the existing monuments, in all probability, will receive park status when their development as parks is practicable. Several of the present parks of the system originally had monument status, notably Grand Canyon, Lafayette, and Zion Parks.

The Parks and Monuments Prior to 1916. From the setting-aside of the Yellowstone Park in 1872 until 1890 no new parks were added to the park system. Sequoia, Yosemite, and General Grant parks were added in 1890, and by the time the National Park Service was created in August, 1916, the system totalled sixteen parks and eighteen monuments. This includes the Hot Springs Reservation, and one park, Casa Grande, which was given monument status in 1918.

The history of the parks and monuments during this period is almost altogether a history of individual rather than group development. New parks and monuments were created from time to time and became, thereupon, so many new individual problems rather than parts of a general problem. No noteworthy legislation of a general nature applying to the park system in common was enacted during this period except the act for the preservation of American antiquities. There was, moreover, no such thing within the Department of the Interior as a section or division charged with the administration of the park system to the exclusion of everything else. The Patents and Miscellaneous Division, in the office of the Secretary, already occupied with an abundance of other duties, gave such attention to the parks as time could be found for. It cannot be said that such a thing as a park system existed, if the word system be used in the sense of a disciplined, coördinated unit. Every park was in a very real sense a law unto itself, and the parks were more of a conglomeration at this time than a system. When the Secretary's office was reorganized in 1907, the miscellaneous duties of this division were given to the Miscellaneous Section in the Secretary's office, and the former chief of division was placed in charge of the section as Assistant Attorney. The work of this section embraced, besides the management of the parks and monuments, the administration of Alaska and Hawaii, the care of several eleemosynary institutions, etc.

A series of national park conferences held in 1911, 1912, and 1915 at the Yellowstone, Yosemite, and Berkeley, California, respectively, and participated in by all the park superintendents and many of the department officers concerned in park administration, had much to do with bringing about an improved system of park control in the department.[3]

The first step in this direction was made in 1913, when Secretary Lane placed the Assistant to the Secretary in general charge of park administration. This was followed, June 5, 1914, by the appointment of a General Superintendent and Landscape Engineer of the national parks, to reside at San Francisco and have general supervision over all the park superintendents. Thereafter a still further advance was made when

---

[3] A fourth conference, held in Washington, January 2-6, 1917, was in the nature of a celebration of the success of the movement for a national park service.

the urgent deficiency appropriation act of February 28, 1916 (39 Stat. L., 23) conferred authority upon the Secretary to employ a General Superintendent in the District of Columbia and in the field, the salary of the new officer and other necessary expenses of administration to be taken from the appropriations and revenues of the several parks on a pro rata basis. Under this authority the office of the General Superintendent was moved to Washington. In the sundry civil appropriation act of July 1, 1916, (39 Stat. L., 309) authorization was given for the employment of a General Superintendent, together with such clerical or other assistants, not exceeding four persons, as the Secretary might determine.

In December 1913, a piece of legislation was enacted which, while it directly affected but one park, the Yosemite, was of indirect effect upon the entire system by reason of the precedent which it established. This was the law (Act of December 19, 1913; 38 Stat. L., 242) giving to the City of San Francisco the right to use certain lands in the Yosemite Park, specifically the Hetch Hetchy Valley, for the construction of a reservoir to supply the city with water and to generate electric power.

This legislation was only enacted after a struggle extending over the better part of a decade. It was fought by many civic organizations of standing and was strongly opposed by naturalists of note like John Muir and by many citizens, who believed that that part of the national park idea which called for the preservation of the parks in their original state should be rigidly lived up to.

The city, on the other hand, claimed that the water to be obtained from the project was essential to the city's life in the years to come, and that it was impracticable to obtain it from any other source. Its point of view finally triumphed. As to whether this triumph was a rightful one; and as to whether it will be a precedent for commercial raiding of the parks, or an example constituting a warning against that danger are questions for the future to answer.

HISTORY

The Movement for the Establishment of the National Park Service. A number of years before Secretary Lane introduced the reforms in park administration which have been described in the preceding section, a feeling had been growing up among friends of the parks that they should be administered by a special bureau devoting its time to park affairs and nothing else. Secretary Lane's innovations were hailed as strides in the right direction, but it was felt that they did not go far enough.

Secretary Ballinger had recommended the creation of a "bureau of national parks and resorts under the supervision of a competent commissioner" in his annual report for 1910. The American Civic Association, a society which has always been active in any movement for park betterment, took up the cause of a park bureau at about the same time. It is not too much to say that the untiring zeal of this organization in keeping up interest in the project, both in and out of Congress, by meetings, publications, and influence brought to bear through the most powerful press organs, had more to do with the final successful issue of the movement than any other one factor. Sentiment in general was in favor of the creation of the bureau, but it was not organized and was largely passive. But for the life the American Civic Association put into the movement it is to be doubted if Congress could have been induced to create a new bureau to do work that had been getting done somehow for so long a time without it.

Another important factor in this movement was the series of national park conferences already referred to. At these meetings of practical park men, with a practical understanding of park problems, the park bureau project found many champions.

What may be termed the "Canadian Argument" was much used by proponents of the bureau idea throughout the movement. It was pointed out that Canada had already established a bureau of parks which was functioning with brilliant success. Secretaries Fisher and Lane were both in favor of the creation of the bureau and recommended it in their reports. President Taft thought well enough of it to address a special message to Congress on the subject. This was afterwards incorporated in a bulletin of the American Civic Association and given wide publicity. President Taft said in part:

> I earnestly recommend the establishment of a bureau of national parks. Such legislation is essential to the proper management of those wondrous manifestations of nature. Every consideration of patriotism and the love of nature and of beauty and of art requires us to expend money enough to bring all these natural wonders within easy reach of our people. The first step in that direction is the establishment of a responsible bureau which shall take upon itself the burden of supervising the parks and of making recommendations as to the best methods of improving their accessibility and usefulness.

The work of the Division of Publications in the Secretary's office was also of material assistance in the bureau campaign. Its annual circulars on each park were widely distributed, and as a knowledge of what the country possessed in the parks became disseminated, sentiment in favor of their more efficient management was crystallized. The issuance by the division in 1916, of an elaborate illustrated brochure entitled The National Parks Portfolio, in an edition of 275,000 copies, aroused popular interest in the parks, and copies of the publication were eagerly sought. The result of this well-directed campaign was the introduction of a number of bills in Congress providing for the creation of a national park service. Hearings were held before the Public Lands committees in 1912, 1914, and 1916, and on August 25, 1916, the National Park Service Act became a law (39 Stat. L., 535).

The National Park Service Since 1916. The text of the National Park Service law will be found in the appendix. The law as originally enacted is in force to-day except for two slight amendments. The first of these is a mere proviso in the act of February 26, 1919 (40 Stat. L., 1175), creating

HISTORY

the Grand Canyon National Park, to the effect that the provision of the original law with regard to the granting of privileges, leases, and permits shall, in the case of the Grand Canyon Park, be so construed that such privileges, leases, etc., "shall be let at public auction to the best and most responsible bidder." The second amendment is part of the act of June 2, 1920 (41 Stat. L., 731), accepting, on the part of the National Government, the cession by the State of California, of jurisdiction over Sequoia, Yosemite, and General Grant Parks. A clause of that act makes a change in the penalties provided in the original act for violation of rules and regulations established by the Secretary of the Interior.

Since the creation of the service in August, 1916, four new parks and five new monuments have been added to the system, which now totals nineteen parks and twenty-four monuments, with a total area of 12,674 square miles. A table of all the parks, together with a map, will be found near the end of this section. A table of the monuments is given with the section on the national monuments.

One of these new monuments, Casa Grande, originally had the status of a park, as has been mentioned above. The reason for making the change cannot be better explained than by quoting from the report of the Director of the National Park Service for 1918, as follows:

When the National Park Service was organized we had 17 national parks and 21 national monuments. We now have 16 national parks and 24 national monuments. The explanation is that one of the national parks of 1916, Casa Grande ruin, has been withdrawn from that classification and been made a national monument, and two other national monuments have been created. . . . The Casa Grande ruin had been reserved [4] and became loosely classed with Hot Springs and Yellowstone as a national park, notwithstanding that it possessed none

---

[4] By an Executive Order of June 22, 1892, authorized by a clause in the sundry civil act of March 2, 1889 (25 Stat. L., 961) which also appropriated $2000 for the restoration of the ruin. A proclamation by President Taft, Dec. 10, 1909 (36 Stat. L., 2504), correcting Casa Grande's boundaries refers to it as a "reservation."

of the accepted qualities of parkhood. . . . President Wilson's proclamation of August 3, 1918 (40 Stat. L., 1818), declaring it a national monument, does little more than confirm one of several opinions.

Projects are now on foot looking to the creation of several additional parks. Prominent among these proposed parks are the region including the Mammoth Cave of Kentucky, a large area in the sand dune region of Indiana bordering on Lake Michigan, and the region in Utah surrounding Bryce Canyon. It is also proposed to enlarge the Yellowstone by taking in a large territory south of the park—the famous country of the Three Tetons and Jackson's Hole—and Sequoia by annexing the contiguous area, which contains the canyons of the King and Kern rivers and about seventy miles of the crest of the Sierra Nevada. This region is notable for scenic grandeur and for the location within its confines of Mount Whitney, the highest peak in the continental United States. It is also the only known habitat of a unique and peculiarly "game" species of trout recently named after the late President Roosevelt. This project is regarded by the National Park Service as the most meritorious of all the projects for park enlargement so far put forward.

By Executive Orders of July 8, 1918 (No. 2905) and January 28, 1921 (No. 3394), the area of the proposed addition to the Yellowstone was set aside and reserved from settlement under authority of the act of June 25, 1910 (36 Stat. L., 847), as amended by the act of August 24, 1912 (37 Stat. L., 497). This prevents the acquisition of any private interests in the tract reserved—except mining claims. The total area withdrawn covers 844,800 acres, of which only slightly over 5000 acres are patented or in process of being patented.

The National Park Service Act constitutes the organic law of the park system. The policy of the National Park Service operating under it was set forth on May 13, 1918, by the late Secretary Lane in a letter to Director Mather, in which he said:

HISTORY

The National Park Service has been established as a bureau of this Department just one year. During this period our efforts have been chiefly directed toward the building of an effective organization while engaged in the performance of duties relating to the administration, protection, and improvement of the national parks and monuments, as required by law. This constructive work is now completed. The new Service is fully organized; its personnel has been carefully chosen; it has been conveniently and comfortably situated in the new Interior Department Building; and it has been splendidly equipped for the quick and effective transaction of its business.

For the information of the public, an outline of the administrative policy to which the new Service will adhere may now be announced. This policy is based on three broad principles: First, that the national parks must be maintained in absolutely unimpaired form for the use of future generations as well as those of our own time; second, that they are set apart for the use, observation, health, and pleasure of the people; and third, that the national interest must dictate all decisions affecting public or private enterprise in the parks.

Every activity of the Service is subordinate to the duties imposed upon it to faithfully preserve the parks for posterity in essentially their natural state. The commercial use of these reservations, except as specially authorized by law, or such as may be incidental to the accommodation and entertainment of visitors, will not be permitted under any circumstances.

In all of the national parks except Yellowstone you may permit the grazing of cattle in isolated regions not frequented by visitors, and where no injury to the natural features of the parks may result from such use. The grazing of sheep, however, must not be permitted in any national park.

In leasing lands for the operation of hotels, camps, transportation facilities, or other public service under strict Government control, concessioners should be confined to tracts no larger than absolutely necessary for the purposes of their business enterprises.

You should not permit the leasing of park lands for summer homes. It is conceivable, and even exceedingly probable, that within a few years under a policy of permitting the establishment of summer homes in national parks, these reservations might become so generally settled as to exclude the public from convenient access to their streams, lakes, and other natural features, and thus destroy the very basis upon which this national playground system is being constructed.

You should not permit the cutting of trees except where timber is needed in the construction of buildings or other improvements within the park and can be removed without injury to the forests or disfigurement of the landscape, where the thinning of forests or cutting of vistas will improve the scenic features of the parks, or where their destruction is necessary to eliminate insect infestations or diseases common to forests and shrubs.

In the construction of roads, trails, buildings, and other improvements, particular attention must be devoted always to the harmonizing of these improvements with the landscape. This is a most important item in our program of development and requires the employment of trained engineers who either possess a knowledge of landscape architecture or have a proper appreciation of the æsthetic value of park lands. All improvements will be carried out in accordance with a preconceived plan developed with special reference to the preservation of the landscape, and comprehensive plans for future development of the national parks on an adequate scale will be prepared as funds are available for this purpose.

Whenever the Federal Government has exclusive jurisdiction over national parks, it is clear that more effective measures for the protection of the parks can be taken. The Federal Government has exclusive jurisdiction over the national parks in the States of Arkansas, Oklahoma, Wyoming, Montana, Washington, and Oregon, and also in the territories of Hawaii and Alaska. We should urge the cession of exclusive jurisdiction over the parks in the other States, and particularly in California [5] and Colorado.

There are many private holdings in the national parks, and many of these seriously hamper the administration of these reservations. All of them should be eliminated as far as it is practicable to accomplish this purpose in the course of time, either through Congressional appropriation or by acceptance of donations of these lands. Isolated tracts in important scenic areas should be given first consideration, of course, in the purchase of private property.

[5] See act of June 2, 1920, p. 104 infra.

HISTORY

Every opportunity should be afforded the public, wherever possible, to enjoy the national parks in the manner that best satisfies the individual taste. Automobiles and motorcycles will be permitted in all of the national parks; in fact, the parks will be kept accessible by any means practicable.

All outdoor sports which may be maintained consistently with the observation of the safeguards thrown around the national parks by law will be heartily endorsed and aided wherever possible. Mountain climbing, horse-back riding, walking, motoring, swimming, boating, and fishing will ever be the favorite sports. Winter sports will be developed in the parks that are accessible throughout the year. Hunting will not be permitted in any national park. [6]

The educational, as well as the recreational, use of the national parks should be encouraged in every practicable way. University and high school classes in science will find special facilities for their vacation period studies. Museums containing specimens of wild flowers, shrubs, and trees, and mounted animals, birds, and fish native to the parks, and other exhibits of this character, will be established as authorized.

Low-priced camps operated by concessioners should be maintained, as well as comfortable and even luxurious hotels wherever the volume of travel warrants the establishment of these classes of accommodations. In each reservation, as funds are available, a system of free camp sites will be cleared, and these grounds will be equipped with adequate water and sanitation facilities.

As concessions in the national parks represent in most instances a large investment, and as the obligation to render service satisfactory to the Department at carefully regulated rates is imposed, these enterprises must be given a large measure of protection, and generally speaking competitive business should not be authorized where a concession is meeting our requirements, which, of course, will as nearly as possible coincide with the needs of the traveling public.

All concessions should yield revenue to the Federal Government, but the development of the revenues of the parks should not impose a burden upon the visitor.

Automobile fees in the parks should be reduced as the volume of motor travel increases.

For assistance in the solution of administrative problems in

[6] But see p. 53, infra.

the parks relating both to their protection and use, the scientific bureaus of the Government offer facilities of the highest worth and authority. In the protection of the public health, for instance, the destruction of insect pests in the forests, the care of wild animals, and the propagation and distribution of fish, you should utilize their hearty coöperation to the utmost.

You should utilize to the fullest extent the opportunity afforded by the Railroad Administration in appointing a committee of western railroads to inform the traveling public how to comfortably reach the national parks; you should diligently extend and use the splendid coöperation developed during the last three years among chambers of commerce, tourist bureaus, and automobile highway associations for the purpose of spreading information about our national parks and facilitating their use and enjoyment; you should keep informed of park movements and park progress, municipal, county, and State, both at home and abroad, for the purpose of adapting, whenever practicable, the world's best thought to the needs of the national parks. You should encourage all movements looking to outdoor living. In particular you should maintain close working relationship with the Dominion Parks Branch of the Canadian Department of the Interior, and assist in the solution of park problems of an international character.

The Department is often requested for reports on pending legislation proposing the establishment of new national parks or the addition of lands to existing parks. Complete data on such parks projects should be obtained by the National Park Service and submitted to the Department in tentative form of report to Congress.

In studying new park projects, you should seek to find scenery of supreme and distinctive quality or some natural feature so extraordinary or unique as to be of national interest and importance. You should seek distinguished examples of typical forms of world architecture; such, for instance, as the Grand Canyon, as exemplifying the highest accomplishment of stream erosion, and the high, rugged portion of Mount Desert Island as exemplifying the oldest rock forms in America and the luxuriance of deciduous forests.

The national park system as now constituted should not be lowered in standard, dignity, and prestige by the inclusion of areas which express in less than the highest terms the particular class or kind of exhibit which they represent.

HISTORY

It is not necessary that a national park should have a large area. The element of size is of no importance as long as the park is susceptible of effective administration and control.

You should study existing national parks with the idea of improving them by the addition of adjacent areas which will complete their scenic purposes or facilitate administration. The addition of the Teton Mountains to the Yellowstone National Park, for instance, will supply Yellowstone's greatest need, which is an uplift of glacier-bearing peaks; and the addition to the Sequoia National Park of the Sierra summits and slopes to the north and east, as contemplated by pending legislation, will create a reservation unique in the world, because of its combination of gigantic trees, extraordinary canyons, and mountain masses.

In considering projects involving the establishment of new national parks or the extension of existing park areas by delimination of national forests, you should observe what effect such delimination would have on the administration of adjacent forest lands, and wherever practicable you should engage in an investigation of such park projects jointly with officers of the Forest Service, in order that questions of national park and national forest policy as they affect the lands involved may be thoroughly understood.

The fundamental purpose of the park system is stated in the National Park Service Act to be the conservation of the scenery and natural and historic objects and wild life of the parks in such manner as will leave them unimparied for the enjoyment of future generations. This thought was emphasized by Secretary Lane in his statement of policy quoted above. It is the gist of the national park idea.

Particular attention is drawn to this matter here because in the few years since the Service has been established events have occurred which indicate that it will be the center about which will be refought, on a much larger scale, the struggle which occurred over the Hetch Hetchy, referred to in the preceding section. Proponents of power, irrigation, and water supply projects want to get in the parks, claiming that local needs along these lines should outweigh other considerations.

In his most recent report Director Mather draws attention to the fact that no less than five extensive irrigation power projects proposing to utilize the waters of Yellowstone lakes and rivers by impounding them within the park itself have been vigorously furthered by Idaho, Montana, and Wyoming interests since 1919, and that one of them had got before Congress and secured a favorable vote in the Senate. It is the opinion of the Director, after careful investigations, that any one of these projects, if completed, would seriously mar the beauty of the park.

A still more serious menace to the National Park Idea was contained in the Federal Water Power Act, signed by President Wilson on June 10, 1920 (41 Stat. L., 1063). This act, when submitted to the National Park Service in tentative form, safeguarded the parks and monuments from commercial invasion for water power or irrigation purposes; but as finally passed by Congress it contained a provision specifically opening up all the parks and monuments for water power development. Upon protest being made, the bill was signed with the understanding that amendatory legislation would be presented and passed at the next session of Congress excluding the parks and monuments from the scope of the act. This action was taken, and an act repealing so much of the Federal Water Power Act as authorized the use of existing parks and monuments for power projects was signed on March 3, 1921 (41 Stat. L., 1353). The parks were further safeguarded from the operation of the act by the inclusion of a clause in the sundry civil act of March 4, 1921 (41 Stat. L., 1380), providing that no part of the appropriation for the Federal Power Commission should be used for any expense connected with the leasing of water power facilities in any national park or monument.

Between the passage of the Water Power Act and its amendment several applications were made to the Federal Power Commission for licenses for water power rights in the Sequoia, Yosemite, and Grand Canyon parks. The commission, however, at the solicitation of the Secretary of the Interior, agreed not to consider applications for licenses within the parks until Congress had an opportunity to enact the promised amendatory legislation.

The successors of the late Secretary Lane have taken a like stand with regard to park exploitation. One of the last utterances of Judge John Barton Payne before relinquishing the Secretaryship of the Interior was the following:

> In my view the greatest assets, stated with reasonable limitations, of the country are such national monuments and parks as the Yellowstone, the Grand Canyon and other national parks which the Congress from time to time has set aside. If those parks may be encroached upon for a commercial purpose, sooner or later they will be destroyed, in my view. It ought not to be a question of utility. Congress presumably considered that when it set a park aside. No one feels more keenly than I the wisdom of conserving water for reclamation and power purposes, but that should not be done at the cost of any of our national parks or monuments. And where the question is one even for debate, every doubt should be resolved in favor of the integrity of the national parks.
>
> The water never remains in the park, and in the final analysis it is a question of expense, because without exception, so far as I know, there is always opportunity of using the water after it leaves the park.
>
> Now, on the Yellowstone project, I gave a hearing to gentlemen when I was in the Yellowstone last July, and we had a perfectly frank dicussion of the subject, and it finally came to the proposition that the project could not afford the cost unless the free lands in the park could be used for that purpose; that to buy the land for a storage reservoir, and pay the damages incident thereto, would make a burden on the reclamation project which it could ill afford to bear. I said that that should not be a question for debate. If the project cannot afford to bear the expense of acquiring new lands and pay the damages, then the project should be abandoned, if the converse of the proposition was the possible injury and destruction of a national park.
>
> The Yellowstone is worth more to this country, it is worth more to Montana and Idaho and Wyoming than any utilitar-

ian use to which it may be applied. It is not only an asset for those adjacent states but for the whole country, and will attract people to that section always, and Congress and the people in the country should do everything in their power to preserve it in the best possible state as a national asset.

And what I feel about Yellowstone is my view about all these parks.

Secretary Fall on June 1, 1921, wrote as follows to the Chairman of the Senate Committee on Irrigation and Reclamation:

I am in receipt of your request for report upon S. 274 and 275, proposing to authorize the State of Montana, or irrigation districts authorized by the State, to build a dam across Yellowstone River at a point not more than three miles below the outlet of Lake Yellowstone, for the regulation of the waters of the Lake for irrigation purposes. This construction would be within the limits of the Yellowstone National Park.

I can not favor the enactment of the measure. I do not believe it would be advisable for Congress to permit private interests to develop irrigation or power sites within the limits of existing national parks. These parks were created by Congress for the preservation of the scenery, forests, and other objects of beauty and interest in their natural condition, and they are created and maintained for general and national purposes as contradistinguished from local development.

If cases be found where it is necessary and advisable in the public interest to develop power and irrigation possibilities in national parks, and it can be done without interference with the purposes of their creation, I am of the opinion that it should only be permitted to be done, whether through the use of private or public funds, on specific authorization by Congress, the works to be constructed and controlled by the Federal Government.

Local feeling on this question is illustrated by the action taken by the Idaho legislature at its 1921 session.[1] For many years the park officers both in Washington and at the several parks, have urged state legislation creating large game pre-

[1] Idaho Senate Bill 173, approved March 1, 1921.

serves immediately adjoining several of the parks, which from their size and location, are especially important wild-life refuges. This applied with especial force to the Yellowstone. The desirability of such legislation is apparent. Certain protected animals, especially the elk and buffalo herds of the Yellowstone, are prone to wander at certain seasons beyond the park boundaries, seeking fresh grazing grounds, and frequently they have been met by hunters and indiscriminately slaughtered. Serious depletion of the park's herds has resulted.

At the last session of the Idaho legislature a game preserve was created approximately seven miles wide, and running from nearly opposite the southwest corner of the park northward to the Continental Divide and the Idaho-Montana line. The act, however, contains the proviso that the preserve shall not be closed to hunting and actually made a sanctuary until the National Government certifies that the southwest corner of the park is made available for irrigation reservoirs, or until the boundaries of the park are so revised as to eliminate the southwest corner and thus make it available for irrigation projects.

The other states bordering on the Yellowstone, Wyoming, and Montana, also passed game preserve legislation at their 1921 legislative sessions. In both states new fish and game commissions were created with broad powers, including the authority to establish game preserves in any parts of their respective states, whenever, in their judgment, such action is advisable. The Montana law, however, is practically nullified by the provision that the commission cannot establish a game preserve unless the same is petitioned for by 75 per cent of the actual property owners of the district proposed to be set aside as a preserve.

A large game preserve was created by the State of Colorado in 1919, enclosing the Rocky Mountain Park on three sides, the fourth being closed by the Continental Divide.

The State of Washington has passed a law somewhat similar to the Montana and Wyoming laws. Under its provisions county game commissioners can set aside as game preserves any state, school, or granted lands, certain designated waters, private lands (with the consent of the owners), and national forest areas (with the consent of the Chief Forester of the United States).

An important bit of park legislation was enacted June 5, 1920 (41 Stat. L., 917) in the shape of a general authorization to the Secretary of the Interior to accept for the National Government, in his discretion, gifts of patented lands or other lands, buildings or other properties within the various national parks and monuments, and moneys which may be donated for the purposes of the national park and monument system. This provision supersedes several clauses in the sundry civil act of June 12, 1917 (40 Stat. L., 152), authorizing acceptances by the Secretary of gifts in Glacier, Mt. Rainier, Mesa Verde, Rocky Mountain, and Crater Lake, as well as gifts of lands etc., including the upper slopes of Grandfather Mountain, near the Boone National Forest in Western North Carolina, a region which after having been under consideration for park purposes for several years has been rejected as unsuitable after a careful examination by the National Park Service.

Under this authorization a number of gifts have been made to the nation within the past year, the latest being a square mile of forest land in the Sequoia Park, the last redwood stand there which had been privately owned. This was secured and handed over to the National Park Service at a cost of $55,000 through the instrumentality of the National Geographic Society.

Another important event having to do with privately-owned land within park boundaries was the termination, in the Government's favor, of long-drawn-out litigation over some mining claims in the Grand Canyon. The decision of the United States Supreme Court in this case [1] established the proposition that the Government can, in the public interest, examine mining claims in the national parks and monuments with a view to determining their validity, and, in the event of their prov-

---

[1] Cameron et al vs, United States; 252 U. S., 450

ing to be non-mineral, declare them invalid, thus preventing the holding of lands within a park on the pretext that they are mineral-bearing.

By act approved June 2, 1920 (41 Stat. L., 731), Congress accepted the cession by the State of California of exclusive jurisdiction of the territory within Yosemite, Sequoia, and General Grant Parks. The state act was passed April 15, 1919. This was an important step toward complete national jurisdiction in all the national parks, which consummation will alone create a satisfactory situation throughout the park system with regard to the enforcement of the regulations. In the parks over which the laws of the state in which they are located obtain, great difficulties in administration are at times encountered, owing to the fact that the department has no jurisdiction to punish offenses in violation of the regulations relating thereto, and particularly in the matter of preventing depredations on the game. Exclusive national jurisdiction now exists in nine parks Yellowstone, Yosemite, Sequoia, General Grant, Platt, Glacier, Mount Rainier, Crater Lake, and Hot Springs. Penalties for the violation of the laws and regulations have been prescribed for all these parks, and commissioners appointed for the trial of offenders in each one of them except Platt.

The period since the creation of the National Park Service is also notable for the assumption by the Department of the Interior of complete control of all activities connected with the park system. This was brought about by the final relinquishment by the War Department of police duties which it had performed for a considerable period in the California parks and in the Yellowstone, and by the withdrawal of the Corps of Engineers from all connection with park road and trail construction. The last detachment of soldiers to garrison Fort Yellowstone was withdrawn from the park on October 31, 1918, and the Corps of Engineers was relieved of further duty in connection with the road work on July 1st of the same year. On July 19th of the following year the engineers were withdrawn from Crater Lake, and the control of the park service was at last complete throughout the entire system. These changes were effected by transference of appropriations in the sundry civil acts of 1918 and 1919 (40 Stat. L., 634, and 41 Stat. L., 163). This finally ended what had always been an anomalous situation, involving a duplication and even a triplication of control. For example, in the Yellowstone the Superintendent reported to the National Park Service and had no control over the commandant of the troops engaged in patrol work or the engineer officer in charge of road construction. The commandant reported to the Western Military Department at San Francisco, and the engineer officer to the Chief of Engineers of the Army. It was thus necessary to maintain at the park three distinct offices, three office forces, and separate warehouses for equipment and supplies.

A word is in order here as to how this cumbersome system grew up. The organic acts creating the Yellowstone Park and the three parks in California (17 Stat. L., 32; 26 Stat. L., 478, 650) gave the Secretary of the Interior power to make rules and regulations, but no means of enforcing them. Considerable disorder and license resulted, and Congress met the situation by including in the act of March 3, 1883 (22 Stat. L., 626) a clause authorizing the Secretary of the Interior to call upon the Secretary of War for details of troops for protection of the Yellowstone. A similar clause was incorporated in the act of June 6, 1900 (31 Stat. L., 618) with regard to the Sequoia, General Grant, and Yosemite parks in California. The same act (31 Stat. L., 625) in making appropriations for the Yellowstone Park under the War Department provided that thereafter road extensions and improvements in the park should be made under, and in harmony with, a plan to be approved by the Chief of Engineers. Engineer troops and officers came to be employed in some of the other parks, notably Crater Lake and Mount Rainier, simply by the making of appropriations for road construction

HISTORY 27

work under the War Department instead of the Interior Department.

This system was probably unavoidable in the early days of the parks, and probably saved the Yellowstone from injury. But as time went on it became more and more apparent that a system of civilian control was to be preferred. Then, too, it was most unjust to the Army. Vast appropriations charged to the War Department were really expended for the benefit of the Department of the Interior. Secretary Garrison on May 1, 1914, called this to the attention of Secretary Lane in a letter reviewing the matter, and suggested that the time had come for the Department of the Interior to take over the complete handling of the parks.

The military forces were withdrawn from the Yellowstone in October, 1916, and a special ranger force created to take over the work. A year later, however, Congress concluded that the park should be guarded by soldiers, and by making Interior Department funds non-available for protective purposes through legislation in the act of June 12, 1917 (40 Stat. L., 151) made necessary the recall of the cavalry to the park. The troops were withdrawn definitely from the California parks in 1913. With the final withdrawal from the Yellowstone in 1918 all military control ceased, and all the parks are now protected by civilian rangers. The system of ranger control is described in the chapter on Organization.

Other events of importance in recent park history have been an inspection trip of a number of members of the House Committee on Appropriations to six of the leading northern parks in the summer of 1920, and the formal establishment and designation of a great connected highway between the major parks of the Far West to be known as the National Park-to-Park Highway.

Mention of this highway leads naturally to mention of the automobile, the basic motive for the creation of the road being the desire for the establishment of a trunk line for motor vehicles that will take the auto tourists to every one of the greater parks of the Far West. The proposal has the approval of the American Automobile Association and the support of the National Park Service.

There was much argument, pro and con, before the automobile was permitted to enter the parks in the early years of Secretary Lane's incumbency. Those opposed to its admission held that to do so would be a violation of the National Park Idea in that it would be an essential ignoring of that part of the "Idea" which contemplated the retention of the parks in their original condition. It was argued on the other hand, that the admission of the auto would render the parks more accessible to the people and thus make of them to a much fuller extent "public parks and pleasuring-grounds." There seems to be no question that a great and ever-increasing number of people are visiting the parks in this manner, as an examination of the statistics in the appendix will disclose. Moreover, the automobile has been a most important revenue-producer. Director Mather stated at the sundry civil hearings of December 16, 1920, that about 60 per cent of the revenue collected in the parks during the fiscal year ending June 30, 1920, came from this source.

In the construction of this highway it is proposed that the eleven states concerned build those sections passing through well-settled portions of their respective territories, and that the National Government assist in constructing those sections traversing thinly populated regions.

The sundry civil act of June 12, 1917 (40 Stat. L., 153) provided that after July 1, 1918, all revenues from national parks except those from Hot Springs should be covered into the Treasury to the credit of miscellaneous receipts. Previous to that time the revenues had been expended in the parks in which earned. The relation of these revenues to the amounts granted by Congress forms an interesting study. The total appropriations for 1920 totalled $907,070.76 and the revenues for the same period totalled $316,877.96, or approximately 35 per cent of the cost of maintenance. The total appropria-

HISTORY

NATIONAL PARKS, ADMINISTERED BY THE NATIONAL PARK SERVICE, DEPARTMENT OF THE INTERIOR
[NUMBER, 19; TOTAL AREA, 10,859 SQUARE MILES; CHRONOLOGICALLY IN ORDER OF CREATION]

Name	Location	When established	Statute Reference L.	Area (square miles)	Area (acres)	Private lands (acres)	Visitors 1920
Hot Springs	Middle Arkansas	Apr. 20, 1832; Mar. 4, 1921	4 Stat. L., 505; 41 Stat. L., 1407	1½	911.63	None	[2] 162,850
Yellowstone	Wyoming, Montana, and Idaho	Mar. 1, 1872	17 Stat. L., 32, 33	3,348	2,142,720	None	79,777
Sequoia (sē-kwoi'á)	Middle eastern California	Sept. 25, 1890	26 Stat. L., 478	252	161,597	2,040	31,508
Yosemite (yŏ-sĕm'ĭ-tē)	......do......	Oct. 1, 1890	26 Stat. L., 650	1,125	719,622.4	10,000	68,906
General Grant	......do......	Oct. 1, 1890	26 Stat. L., 702	4	2,536	160	19,661
Mount Rainier (rā-nēr')	West central Washington	Mar. 2, 1899	30 Stat. L., 993	324	207,360	18.2	56,491
Crater Lake	Southern Oregon	May 22, 1902	32 Stat. L., 202	249	159,360	2,458.11	20,135
Wind Cave	South Dakota	Jan. 9, 1903	32 Stat. L., 765	17	10,899.22	None	27,023
Platt	Southern Oklahoma	{July 1, 1902; Apr. 21, 1904}	32 Stat. L., 641; 33 Stat. L., 220	1⅓	848.22	None	[2] 38,000
Sullys Hill	North Dakota	Apr. 27, 1904	33 Stat. L., 322	1½	780	None	9,341
Mesa Verde (mā'sa vēr'da)	Southwestern Colorado	June 29, 1906	34 Stat. L., 616; 38 Stat. L., 82, 83	77	48,966.4	993	2,890
Glacier (glā'sher)	Northwestern Montana	May 11, 1910	36 Stat. L., 354	1,534	981,681	16,508.1	22,449
Rocky Mountain	North middle Colorado	Jan. 26, 1915	38 Stat. L., 798	397½	254,327	[2] 20,693	[2] 240,966
Hawaii (ha-wī'ē)	Hawaiian Islands	Aug. 1, 1916	39 Stat. L., 432	118	75,295	[2] 41,000	(3)
Lassen Volcanic (lăs'en)	Northern California	Aug. 9, 1916	39 Stat. L., 442	124	79,561.58	2,955	[2] 2,000
Mount McKinley	South central Alaska	Feb. 26, 1917	39 Stat. L., 938	2,200	1,498,000	None	(3)
Grand Canyon [4]	North central Arizona	{Jan. 11, 1908; Feb. 26, 1919}	35 Stat. L., 2175; 40 Stat. L., 1175	958	613,120	732.16	67,315
Lafayette [5]	Maine coast	{July 8, 1916; Feb. 26, 1919}	39 Stat. L., 1785; 40 Stat. L., 1178	8	5,000	None	[2] 66,500
Zion [6]	Southwestern Utah	{Mar. 18, 1918; Nov. 19, 1919}	40 Stat. L., 1760; 41 Stat. L., 356	120	76,800	9,817.72	3,692

[1] In Wyoming, 3,114 square miles; in Montana, 198 square miles; in Idaho, 36 square miles.
[2] Estimated.
[3] No record kept.
[4] Formerly Grand Canyon National Monument.
[5] Formerly Sieur de Monts National Monument; donated to the United States.
[6] Formerly Zion National Monument.

Name	Special characteristics
Hot Springs	46 hot springs, possessing curative properties—Many hotels and boarding houses—20 bathhouses under public control.
Yellowstone	More geysers than in all rest of world together—Boiling springs—Mud volcanoes—Petrified forests—Grand Canyon of the Yellowstone, remarkable for gorgeous coloring—Large lakes—Waterfalls—Vast wilderness inhabited by deer, elk, bison, moose, antelope, bear, mountain sheep, etc.—Greatest wild bird and animal preserve in world.
Sequoia (sē-kwol'á)	The Big Tree National Park—12,000 sequoia trees over 10 feet in diameter, some 25 to 36 feet in diameter—Towering mountain ranges—Startling precipices—Cave of considerable size—Fine trout fishing.
Yosemite (yō-sĕm'-ĭ-tē)	Valley of world-famed beauty—Lofty cliffs—Romantic vistas—Waterfalls of extraordinary height—3 groves of big trees—Large areas of snowy peaks—Waterwheel Falls—Good trout fishing.
General Grant	Created to preserve the celebrated General Grant Tree, 35 feet in diameter—6 miles from Sequoia National Park.
Mount Rainier (rā-nēr')	Largest accessible single peak glacier system—28 glaciers, some of large size—48 square miles of glacier, 50 to 500 feet thick—Wonderful subalpine wild-flower fields.
Crater Lake	Lake of extraordinary blue in crater of extinct volcano, no inlet, no outlet—Sides 1,000 feet high—Interesting lava formations—Fine fishing.
Wind Cave	Cavern having many miles of galleries and numerous chambers of considerable size containing many peculiar formations.
Platt	Many sulphur and other springs possessing medicinal value.
Sullys Hill	Small park with woods, streams, and a lake—Is an important wild-animal preserve.
Mesa Verde (mā'sa vĕr'dä)	Most notable and best preserved prehistoric cliff dwellings in United States, if not in the world.
Glacier (glā'sher)	Rugged mountain region of unsurpassed Alpine character—250 glacier-fed lakes of romantic beauty—60 small glaciers—Precipices thousands of feet deep—Almost sensational scenery of marked individuality—Fine trout fishing.
Rocky Mountain	Heart of the Rockies—Snowy range, peaks 11,000 to 14,250 feet altitude—Remarkable records of glacial period.
Hawaii (ha-wi'e)	3 separate areas:—2—Kilauea, continuously active for century, and Mauna Loa, altitude 13,675 (largest active volcano in the world, erupting every decade)—are on Hawaii; Haleakala, on Maui, 10,000 feet high, with tremendous rift in summit 8 miles across and 3,000 feet deep; contains many cones, gorgeous tropical forests, mahagony groves, and lava caves; erupted 200 years ago.
Lassen Volcanic (las'en)	Only active volcano in United States proper—Lassen peak, 10,465 feet in altitude—Cinder Cone, 6,879 feet—Hot springs—Mud geysers—Ice caves—Majestic canyons—Numerous lakes—Fine forests.
Mount McKinley	Highest mountain in North America (altitude 20,300 feet)—Rises higher above surrounding country than any other mountain in world.
Grand Canyon 4	The greatest example of erosion and the most sublime spectacle in the world.
Lafayette 5	The group of granite mountains upon Mount Desert Island.
Zion 6	Magnificent gorge (Zion Canyon), depth from 800 to 2,000 feet, with precipitous walls.—Of great beauty and scenic interest.

tions for 1921 were $1,058,969.16, with a corresponding revenue of $396,928.27.

The sources of park revenue are four in number: taxes on concessions; public utilities, such as water, telephone, or power systems; natural resources, i. e., sales of dead timber, stone, hides of predatory animals, etc.; and automobile and motorcycle permits. The system of taxing concessions varies in the different parks.

Tables of statistics showing appropriations for the several parks and monuments are given in the Appendix.

The Several Parks. In the pages that follow individual sketches of the parks in the national system are given in some detail.

Yellowstone. The creation of the Yellowstone National Park and the legislation authorizing the same have already been referred to. For more than a decade after its creation little was done for its protection or development. The appropriations were not large, and the lack of support made it impossible for the early superintendents to accomplish much that was genuinely constructive. The first superintendent was the Hon. N. P. Langford, who, as mentioned above, had been a member of the Washburn-Doane expedition. He received no salary, and his hands were so securely tied by lack of funds and lack of means for enforcement of the regulations that he was practically powerless. He was nevertheless severely criticised for his administration.

Civilian administration during these early years proving unsatisfactory, the act of March 3, 1883 (22 Stat. L., 626) made some radical changes. It provided for a civilian superintendent and ten assistants, but the protection of the park was entrusted to a detail of troops which the Secretary of the Interior was authorized to request of the Secretary of War, and the development of roads and bridges was entrusted to the Corps of Engineers of the Army.

The act of August 4, 1886 (24 Stat. L., 240), by making no

provision for a superintendent or assistant, threw the entire administration and protection of the parks into the hands of the military, there being nothing for the Secretary of the Interior to do but call on the Secretary of War for a detail of troops. This practice was thereupon continued from year to year, and the commanding officer of Fort Yellowstone was designated as acting superintendent reporting to the Secretary of the Interior. The soldiers, thereafter, were used not merely for purposes of protection but for general administrative purposes, serving practically as rangers.

After 1888, up to and including 1901, the park appropriations were made directly through the War Department, but expenditures from the park revenues were made by the Secretary of the Interior. After the act of March 2, 1895 (28 Stat. L., 945), under which the War Department appropriations covered protection as well as improvement, expenditures from the revenues could be made for managerial purposes only. Beginning with the act of March 3, 1901 (31 Stat. L., 1169), small appropriations were again made through the Interior Department for administration and protection, out of which clerical help was furnished to the acting superintendent and a few scouts and other additional employees paid.

But the great landmark in Yellowstone legislation, second only to the organic act, was the act of May 7, 1894 (28 Stat. L., 73) which put teeth into the earlier law and enabled the park authorities to enforce the regulations and give the park and its wild life a protection never enjoyed before. The passage of this act was brought about by the capture of a poacher who slaughtered several buffaloes, well knowing that if caught, removal from the park would be the extent of his punishment. This resulted in immediate action by Congress, which passed a law that provided, among other things, for the appointment of a resident United States Commissioner with power to try for misdemeanors, and to issue process and commit in the case of felonies; for summary arrest in case of open violation of the regulations; for the erection of a jail; and for the appoint-

HISTORY

ment of a resident deputy United States marshal. This act was amended and made more practicable by the act of June 28, 1916 (39 Stat. L., 238), which, by modifying the punishments prescribed, made it possible to treat violations as misdemeanors and thus do away with the necessity of formal indictment.

A fact not generally known is that the entire Yellowstone area is not under National jurisdiction. The act of July 10, 1890 (26 Stat. L., 222), admitting Wyoming into the Union retained national jurisdiction over the park area. This law does not apply to the strips of the park located in Montana and Idaho. These strips, however, are of very slight extent, being only a few miles wide. The greater part of the park, fully 95 per cent of the total area, is in Wyoming. The situation, however, is one which contains many possibilities for conflict, especially in regard to game protection, attention to which was called by the Chief Forester in his 1916 report. In the Yellowstone region, comprising the park and adjacent national forests, the game in the park, i. e., in the Wyoming portion of it, is under national jurisdiction, while the game in the forests and in the Idaho and Montana park strips is under state jurisdiction, there being three states with differing laws to reckon with.

That provision of the organic act creating the National Park Service which gives the Secretary of the Interior authority to permit grazing at his discretion in the parks and monuments does not apply to the Yellowstone. No grazing is permitted there.

As has been stated above, the military were finally withdrawn from the Yellowstone in 1918, and entire control since that time has been in the hands of the National Park Service.

Yosemite. Yosemite's history as a park dates back to before the days of the Yellowstone, the valley proper and the Mariposa Big Tree Grove having been granted to the State of California for use as a state park by the act of June 30, 1864 (13 Stat. L., 325). The whole of this park area was surrounded by, but not included in, the area set apart by the act of October 1, 1890 (26 Stat. L., 650) for a national park under the Secretary of the Interior.

The act of April 28, 1904 (33 Stat. L., 478) directed the Secretary of the Interior to ascertain what part of the area set aside by the act of 1890 was not necessary for park purposes and could be returned to the public domain. In the following year, accordingly, certain lands were excluded from the area originally set aside, and the remaining reservation was named the Yosemite National Park (act of February 7, 1905; 33 Stat. L., 702). It was provided, however, that revenues accruing from the lands excluded should go to the park. With the formal acceptance by the United States (Joint resolution of June 11, 1906; 34 Stat. L., 831) of the recession by California of the lands given for a state park in 1864 (California Session Law, March 3, 1905) the creation of the Yosemite as a national park was complete, the lands receded being included in the national park created in 1890.

Beginning with the season of 1891 troops were detailed to guard the park, and this system continued except for short intervals until 1914, when they were withdrawn by agreement. The act of June 6, 1900 (31 Stat. L., 618) directed the Secretary of War to make troop details on request of the Secretary of the Interior. As in the case of the Yellowstone, the commander of the troops was acting superintendent. The troops did not remain in the park during the winter, however, and no permanent post was established.

The act of December 19, 1913 (38 Stat. L., 242) granted the city and county of San Francisco the right to create a reservoir in the Hetch Hetchy Valley in the Yosemite Park for the purpose of supplying the city with water.

The act of June 2, 1920 (41 Stat. L., 731) accepted, on the part of the United States, exclusive jurisdiction in the Yosemite, Sequoia, and General Grant Parks.

Sequoia and General Grant. The acts of September 25,

and October 1, 1890 (26 Stat. L., 478 and 650) set aside, with the usual conditions as to control by the Secretary of the Interior, the making by him of rules and regulations, and the granting of leases, etc., two park areas in California which received the names, respectively of Sequoia and General Grant. The history of these two parks between 1891 and 1914 corresponds exactly to that of the Yosemite during the same period.

By the act of July 1, 1916 (39 Stat. L., 308) there was appropriated the sum of $50,000, which was added to $20,000 contributed by the National Geographic Society, and the whole used to purchase some private holdings in Sequoia Park, which included parts of the Giant Forest. Since then other gifts by the National Geographic Society and certain citizens, totalling over $80,000, have resulted in over a thousand acres of privately owned land in this park being returned to public possession.

As these parks are only a short distance apart, and as the General Grant Park is very small, being only four square miles in extent, they are administered together under one superintendent.

Mount Rainier. This park, which includes within its boundaries the mountain after which it was named and the adjacent territory, was created by the act of March 2, 1899 (30 Stat. L., 993) which differs from the ordinary park-creating act in that it provides for the extension of the mineral land laws to the territory set aside. This provision was nullified, however, by the act of May 27, 1908 (35 Stat. L., 365) which prohibited the location of further claims.

A concession for transportation was allowed in 1902, and the park placed under the supervision of the Forest Supervisor of the State of Washington. Protection has been provided by means of civilian rangers from the first opening of the park, although much of the original road construction was performed by army engineers.

Cession by the State of Washington of exclusive jurisdiction was accepted by the act of June 30, 1916 (39 Stat. L., 243).

Crater Lake. Crater Lake National Park, comprising about 250 square miles in Southwestern Oregon, surrounding the lake of the same name, was created by the act of May 22, 1902 (32 Stat. L., 202). This act corresponds in general to the other park acts, but makes no provision for use of park revenues in the development of the park, as do the acts creating the parks heretofore noticed. Administration and protection have always been performed by civilians, but until 1919 road building was in charge of Army engineers.

Cession of exclusive jurisdiction by Oregon was accepted by the United States by the act of August 21, 1916 (39 Stat. L., 512).

Wind Cave. This park, which includes some 10,000 acres in Southwestern South Dakota, was created by the act of January 9, 1903 (32 Stat. L., 765). By the act of August 12, 1912 (37 Stat. L., 293) part of the park area was constituted a game preserve, and the Secretary of Agriculture was authorized to purchase necessary adjoining lands and enclose and protect the preserve. Several tracts of privately owned land which were inside the park boundaries at the time the park was created have since been acquired by the National Government.

The game preserve is in charge of the Bureau of Biological Survey and includes some 4000 acres, well fenced, on which are maintained herds of buffalo, elk, antelope, and deer.

An Executive Order of July 14, 1920, temporarily withdrew $2\frac{1}{4}$ sections of public land adjoining the park to conserve a water supply for the animal herds.

Platt. This park, known as Sulphur Springs Reservation until the name was changed by joint resolution of June 29, 1906 (34 Stat. L., 837), was created by the act of July 1, 1892 (32 Stat. L., 641, 655). This act confirmed an agreement made with the Choctaw and Chickasaw Indians, and by its provisions a tract of land, to be designated by the Secretary

HISTORY

of the Interior, was relinquished to the United States. By act of April 21, 1904 (33 Stat. L., 220), additions were made to the park, which now comprises approximately 850 acres just outside the town of Sulphur, Oklahoma. The park contains several unique mineral springs and is of considerable natural beauty. It also has a well-fenced game preserve containing several buffaloes and elk. The Enabling Act of June 16, 1906 (34 Stat. L., 267) and the Oklahoma Constitution adopted July 16, 1907 provided for the retention of National jurisdiction over the park area.

Sullys Hill. In the Presidential Proclamation of June 2, 1904 (33 Stat. L., 2368), under the act of April 24, 1904 (33 Stat. L., 319), throwing open the Devils Lake Indian Reservation to settlement, there is incorporated a clause excepting some 780 acres on the south shore of Devils Lake "for public use as a park to be known as Sullys Hill Park." No provision was made for administration, and except for one small appropriation—$500—to determine its mineral or nonmineral qualities, no appropriations have been made for the park through the Department of the Interior. It has become an important game preserve of the Bureau of Biological Survey, however, and has received fairly liberal appropriations for that purpose. Its park uses are mostly in the nature of a local picnic ground.

Mesa Verde. Mesa Verde Park, notable for its prehistoric ruins, was created by the act of June 29, 1906 (34 Stat. L., 616) which, though similar in general form to the average park-creating law, contains a provision authorizing the Secretary of the Interior to grant permits for excavation. In 1909 an attempt was made to amend this act so that the leases and permits granted by the Secretary of the Interior in the park should be restricted to coal mining for local use in Montezuma county, Colorado, the revenue derived therefrom to be covered into the Treasury without right on the part of the Secretary to use it for park development. This act was vetoed by President Taft on April 28, 1910. The park's area was enlarged by the act of June 30, 1913 (38 Stat. L., 82).

Considerable archæological research has been done in the park by the Smithsonian Institution, and the establishment of a school of archæology has been proposed. There is a museum in the park for the display of pottery and other relics of the region.

Glacier. Glacier Park comprises about 1500 square miles in northwestern Montana adjoining the Canadian boundary, and contains within its borders probably the finest Alpine scenery to be found in the United States outside of Alaska. It was created by the act of May 11, 1910 (36 Stat. L., 354). It directly adjoins the Waterton Lakes Park of the Canadian park system, on the north.

Appropriations for this park have been regular and fairly liberal from the date of its foundation, and it has been developed into one of the most important and popular parks of the entire system. Much credit for the development and advertising of the park is due the Great Northern Railway, which has expended between two and three million dollars in the creation of a system of hotels and chalets.

All park activities have been in civilian hands from the first, the military arm never having been called upon for either protection or road construction.

Acceptance from Montana of exclusive jurisdiction was effected by the act of August 22, 1914 (38 Stat. L., 699), and, as in the case of all the other parks, save Platt, in which jurisdiction has been ceded, penalties for violations of the laws and regulations were prescribed, and provision made for a United States Commissioner with jurisdiction over offenses committed within the park.

The act of July 3, 1916 (39 Stat. L., 342) provided that certain homesteaders who had entered upon lands in the park area before the park was created should be protected in their rights, but that in the event of the non-perfecting of the entries the lands covered thereby should revert to the park.

By the act of March 3, 1917 (39 Stat. L., 1122) the Secretary of the Interior was authorized to exchange for private lands held within the park, matured timber of an equal value located either on Government land in the park or in the adjacent national forest in Montana.

Rocky Mountain. Rocky Mountain Park was created by the act of June 26, 1915 (38 Stat. L., 798), the law being similar to the standard park-creating law save for an inhibition upon appropriations of more than $10,000 in any one year except by special Congressional authorization. This proviso was repealed by the act of March 1, 1919 (40 Stat. L., 1271). The park's boundaries were enlarged by the act of February 14, 1917 (39 Stat. L., 916), giving it a total area of about 400 square miles. It is located in north central Colorado.

Hawaii. Hawaii Park is unique for several reasons, one being that it was created on the initiative of Congress by the act of August 1, 1916 (39 Stat. L., 432), the act varying from the standard park law only in that it provided that no appropriation should be made until proper conveyance had been made to the United States of rights of way over private lands to secure access to the park. By the act of February 27, 1920 (41 Stat. L., 452) the Governor of Hawaii was authorized to acquire, at Hawaii's expense, all private lands lying in the park boundaries and all necessary rights of way, etc., thereover. Provision was therefore made by an appropriation of $10,000 in the act of March 4, 1921 (41 Stat. L., 1407) for the necessary administration and protection, which can be effected with a superintendent, clerk, and two rangers. It is the expectation of the National Park Service that this park will speedily become very popular and a good producer of revenue.

Lassen. This park, located in northeastern California, comprises the territory surrounding Mount Lassen, the only active volcano within the limits of the continental United States. It was created by the act of August 9, 1916 (39 Stat. L., 442) which contains an inhibition on appropriations of more than $5,000 without express authorization. Two appropriations have been made, one of $2,500 by the act of June 5, 1920 (41 Stat. L., 918); the other, of $3,000 by the act of March 4, 1921 (41 Stat. L., 1407), arrangements for the expenditure of which sum in the construction of roads and trails have been made with the Forest Service. Forest Service employees of the neighboring Lassen National Forest are giving the park what protection they can. A movement instituted in 1919 to have the park abolished and restored to the forest reserve proved abortive.

Mount McKinley. Mount McKinley Park was created by the act of February 26, 1917 (39 Stat. L., 938). The act does not differ from the other park acts save in that it specifically continues in force the mineral land laws as regards the park area and limits appropriations to $10,000 per annum. No appropriations were made nor anything done to protect the park until March 4, 1921 (41 Stat. L., 1407), when $8,000 was appropriated for its protection. A ranger with one assistant was sent into the park in the Spring of 1921, and a start has thus been made toward protection of the great game herds, which in recent years have been seriously harried by poachers. It is believed that this territory will become as great a game preserve as the Yellowstone.

Grand Canyon. The act of February 26, 1919 (40 Stat. L., 1175) created the Grand Canyon National Park out of a portion of Grand Canyon National Monument in northern Arizona, which had in turn been created by the Presidential Proclamation of June 11, 1908 (35 Stat. L., 2175). The act creating the park is, in general, of the usual form, but contains two unusual provisions: one authorizing the Secretary of the Interior to conduct negotiations with the authorities of Coconino county, Arizona, with a view to the purchase of the Bright Angel Trail, a toll road in the park owned and maintained by the county; the other providing that all concessions, leases, privileges, etc., granted in the park shall be sold at public auction to the highest bidder. It also provides that prospecting is to be allowed in the park at the Secretary's

HISTORY

discretion when not calculated to interfere with the park's primary purpose.

Since the park's establishment, appropriations have been made as follows: July 19, 1919 (41 Stat. L., 204), $40,000; June 5, 1920 (41 Stat. L., 918) $60,000; and March 4, 1921 (41 Stat. L., 1407), $100,000. A clause in the 1920 and 1921 acts provides that no parts of the respective appropriations are to be used for the improvement of any toll road or toll trail, a provision undoubtedly aimed at the Bright Angel Trail. All three appropriations are for "administration, protection, maintenance and improvement" and the first one is for "development" as well. The second, in addition to the objects mentioned, is also for "acquisition of road and trail rights."

Negotiations held so far with Coconino County have come to nothing. The county charges one dollar per person for the use of the trail, and claims that its value based on its earning power is $100,000. The National Park Service, on the other hand, has ascertained that a new trail can be built for $30,000.

Lafayette. This park, comprising some 5000 acres in Mt. Desert Island, off the Maine coast, is notable in being the first park to be established on the Atlantic seaboard. It was first set aside as the Sieur de Monts National Monument by the Proclamation of July 8, 1916 (39 Stat. L., 1785), and later obtained park status by the act of February 26, 1919 (40 Stat. L., 1178), the act being very brief and merely stating that the park was created and was to be administered by the National Park Service. The acts of July 19, 1919 and June 5, 1920 (41 Stat. L., 204 and 918) carried appropriations for Lafayette Park of $10,000 and $20,000, respectively, both for "administration, maintenance, protection and improvement."

Zion. The area included in Zion Park in southwestern Utah was originally set apart as Mukuntuweap National Monument by Proclamation of July 31, 1909 (36 Stat. L., 2498). The Proclamation of March 18, 1918 (40 Stat. L., 1760) enlarged this monument and changed its name to Zion National Monument, which, in the following year, by act of November 19, 1919 (41 Stat. L., 356) became Zion National Park. The act provided that the park should be administered by the National Park Service and maintained by an allotment of funds from the appropriations for the monuments until an independent appropriation should be made. Two appropriations have been made by the acts of June 5, 1920 and March 4, 1921 (41 Stat. L., 919 and 1408), in the respective amounts of $7,500 and $10,000 for "administration, protection, maintenance and improvement."

Hot Springs. Hot Springs Park is unique not only as the "Great American Spa" but as being at once the oldest and the youngest member of the park system. It was reserved many years before any other member of the park system, April 20, 1832 (4 Stat. L., 505), but did not finally receive the name of park until March 4, 1921 (41 Stat. L., 1407). Because of its nature its history has been different from that of every other member of the system. It is a health resort rather than a "pleasure ground." It is only fair to add, however, that the development of Hot Springs in recent years, its equable climate, and the beauty of the surrounding region combine to make it a far from unattractive place to visit.

The act of June 11, 1870 (16 Stat. L., 149) authorized suit in the Court of Claims by any one claiming title to any land in the reservation, and for a receiver to take charge of the lands in case of decision in favor of the United States. Final decision was so rendered by the Supreme Court in October, 1875.[1] By the act of March 3, 1877 (19 Stat. L., 377) a commission was created to lay off the reservation into lots and streets, to set apart Hot Springs Mountain as a permanent reservation and to condemn the buildings thereon, to determine upon the rights of claimants to take lots at appraised values, and to sell the lots not so taken. Hot Springs Mountain was placed in charge of a superintendent to be appointed by the

[1] "Hot Springs Cases," 2 Otto, 698.

Secretary of the Interior. Proceeds from the sale of lots and receipts from water rents were to be devoted to the reservation. The act of December 16, 1878 (20 Stat. L., 258) authorized the Secretary of the Interior to execute leases on the permanent reservation, and directed the superintendent, out of the rentals, to provide free baths for the indigent. The act of June 16, 1880 (21 Stat. L., 288) added the other undivided mountainous districts to the permanent reservation, and ceded the streets and thoroughfares not in the permanent reservation to the town of Hot Springs, a municipal corporation of the State of Arkansas.

The Government Free Bath House was authorized in 1878, and has been enlarged from time to time. In 1920 construction of a new free bath house was begun. Besides the free bath house, there are nineteen pay bath houses in Hot Springs receiving hot water from the park, the rates charged for baths being fixed in each instance by the Secretary of the Interior. Under governmental authority a free clinic was organized in April 1916 in connection with the free bath house.

The act of June 30, 1882 (22 Stat. L., 121) appropriated $100,000 for an Army and Navy Hospital to be erected on the reservation and to be subject to such rules, regulations, and restrictions as might be provided by the President of the United States.

Acceptance was made by act of April 20, 1904 (30 Stat. L., 187) of cession by the State of Arkansas of exclusive jurisdiction over a portion of the permanent reservation on the Hot Springs Mountain. This act was amended by the acts of March 2, 1907 (34 Stat. L., 1218) and March 3, 1911 (36 Stat. L., 1086) so as to make more definite the provision regarding a United States Commissioner.

The National Monuments. Individual sketches of the national monuments would be superfluous. They received no appropriations prior to 1917. Since then, appropriations general and special have totalled $75,500. They were placed in charge of officers of the Department of the Interior in the vicinity—General Land Office employees, etc. In a few cases custodians have been employed at nominal salaries, and in the case of Muir Woods custodian service has been paid out of the appropriation for protecting public lands. Many of the monuments—for example, The Devils Tower in eastern Wyoming—will need no custodians, being practically injury proof. In the case of monuments like the Southwestern Ruins and the Petrified Forest, which are vulnerable to the vandal and despoiler, it is the policy to provide protection. A ranger has recently been placed in the Petrified Forest.

The principal facts relating to the individual monuments are set forth on pages 45 and 46:

Parks and Monuments not Administered by the National Park Service. Although this monograph is concerned primarily with the National Park Service and the parks and monuments under its jurisdiction, brief mention should be made of a number of national parks and monuments under other control. A complete list of them is contained in the tables on pages 47 and 48:

In addition to the parks listed in these tables, there was formerly another national park under the War Department. A portion of Mackinac Island, Michigan, possessed that status from 1875 to 1895, when it was turned over to Michigan for use as a state park.

Of the monuments in these tables, those under the Agriculture Department are all located within the bounds of forest reserves, that being the determining factor which placed them under the Agriculture Department instead of the Interior Department at the time of their creation. A monument may be transferred from the Agriculture Department to the Interior Department at any time by simply revoking the forest reservation covering its area. The military monuments, by the same token, are located on military reservations.

Growth of Popular Interest in the Park System. In 1908

HISTORY

NATIONAL MONUMENTS, ADMINISTERED BY THE NATIONAL PARK SERVICE. DEPARTMENT OF THE INTERIOR
[NUMBER, 24 TOTAL AREA, 1,815 SQUARE MILES; CHRONOLOGICALLY IN ORDER OF CREATION]

Name	Location	Date of creation	Statute reference of proclamation	Area (acres)	Special characteristics
Devils Tower	Wyoming	Sept. 24, 1906	34 Stat. L., 3236	1,152	Remarkable natural rock tower, of volcanic origin, 1,200 feet in height.
Montezuma Castle	Arizona	Dec. 8, 1906	34 Stat. L., 3265	1 160	Prehistoric cliff-dwelling ruin of unusual size situated in a niche in face of a vertical cliff. Of scenic and ethnologic interest.
El Morro	New Mexico	Dec. 8, 1906 June 18, 1917	34 Stat. L., 3264 40 Stat. L., 1673	160 240	Enormous sandstone rock eroded in form of a castle, upon which inscriptions have been placed by early Spanish explorers. Contains cliff-dweller ruins. Of great historic, scenic, and ethnologic interest.
Petrified Forest	Arizona	Dec. 8, 1906 July 31, 1911	34 Stat. L., 3266 37 Stat. L., 1716	25,625	Abundance of petrified coniferous trees, one of which forms a small natural bridge. Is of great scientific interest.
Chaco Canyon (chä′kō)	New Mexico	Mar. 11, 1907	35 Stat. L., 2119	1 20,629	Numerous cliff-dweller ruins, including communal houses, in good condition and but little excavated.
Muir Woods 2 (mūr)	California	Jan. 9, 1908 Sept. 22, 1921	35 Stat. L., 2174 42 Stat. L., 1608	295 423.14	One of the most noted redwood groves in California, and was donated by Hon. William Kent, ex-Member of Congress. Located 7 miles from San Francisco.
Pinnacles	....do	Jan. 16, 1908	35 Stat. L., 2177	2,080	Many spirelike rock formations, 600 to 1,000 feet high, visible many miles; also numerous caves and other formations.
Natural Bridges	Utah	Apr. 16, 1908 Sept. 25, 1909 Feb. 11, 1916	35 Stat. L., 2183 36 Stat. L., 2502 39 Stat. L., 1764	120 1 2,740 1 2,740	3 natural bridges, among largest examples of their kind. Largest bridge is 222 feet high, 65 feet thick at top of arch; arch is 28 feet wide; span, 261 feet; height of span, 157 feet. Other two slightly smaller.
Lewis and Clark Cavern 2	Montana	May 11, 1908 May 16, 1911	35 Stat. L., 2187 37 Stat. L., 1679	160 160	Immense limestone cavern of great scientific interest, magnificently decorated with stalactite formations. Now closed to public because of depredations by vandals.
Tumacacori (tū-mä-kä′kō-rē)	Arizona	Sept. 15, 1908	35 Stat. L., 2205	10	Ruin of Franciscan mission dating from seventeenth century. Being restored by National Park Service as rapidly as funds permit.
Navajo (nāv′a-hō)	....do	Mar. 20, 1909 Mar. 14, 1912	36 Stat. L., 2491 37 Stat. L., 1733	1 600 360	Numerous pueblo, or cliff-dweller ruins, in good preservation.
Shoshone Cavern (shō-shō′nē)	Wyoming	Sept. 21, 1909	36 Stat. L., 2501	210	Cavern of considerable extent, near Cody.

1 Estimated   2 Donated to the United States.

Name	Location	Date	Statute	Area (acres)	Description
Gran Quivira (grän-kē-vē'rä)	New Mexico	Nov. 1, 1909; Nov. 25, 1919	36 Stat. L., 2503; 41 Stat. L., Proc.	a 160	One of the most important of earliest Spanish mission ruins in the Southwest. Monument also contains pueblo ruins.
Sitka	Alaska	1778; Mar. 23, 1910	36 Stat. L., 2601	a 57	Park of great natural beauty, and historic interest as scene of massacre of Russians by Indians. Contains 16 totem poles of best native workmanship.
Rainbow Bridge	Utah	May 30, 1910	36 Stat. L., 2703	160	Unique natural bridge of great scientific interest and symmetry. Height 309 feet above water, and span is 278 feet, in shape of rainbow.
Colorado	Colorado	May 24, 1911	37 Stat. L., 1681	13,883	Many lofty monoliths, and is wonderful example of erosion, and of great scenic beauty and interest.
Papago Saguaro (pä'pä-gō sä-gwä'rō)	Arizona	Jan. 31, 1914	38 Stat. L., 1991	2,050	Splendid collection of characteristic desert flora and numerous pictographs. Interesting rock formations.
Dinosaur (dī'nō-sor)	Utah	Oct. 4, 1915	39 Stat. L., 1752	80	Deposits of fossil remains of prehistoric animal life of great scientific interest.
Capulin Mountain (kä-pū'lin)	New Mexico	Aug. 9, 1916	39 Stat. L., 1792	681	Cinder cone of geologically recent formation.
Verendrye (vĕr-rŏn-drē)	North Dakota	June 29, 1917	40 Stat. L., 1677	253.04	Includes Crowhigh Butte, peculiar mountain formation, from which Explorer Verendrye first beheld territory beyond Missouri River.
Casa Grande (kä'sä grän'dā)	Arizona	Mar. 2, 1889; b Dec. 10, 1909; Aug. 3, 1918	25 Stat. L., 961; 36 Stat. L., 2504; 40 Stat. L., 1818	480	These ruins are one of the most noteworthy relics of a prehistoric age and people within the limits of the United States. Discovered in ruinous condition in 1694.
Katmai (kăt'mī)	Alaska	Sept. 24, 1918	40 Stat. L., 1855	a 1,088,000	Wonderland of great scientific interest in the study of volcanism. Phenomena exist upon a scale of great magnitude. Includes "Valley of Ten Thousand Smokes."
Scotts Bluff	Nebraska	Dec. 12, 1919	41 Stat. L., 1781	2,053.83	Region of historic and scientific interest. Many famous old trails traversed by the early pioneers in the winning of the West passed over and through this monument.
Yucca house c (yuc'cä)	Colorado	Dec. 19, 1919	41 Stat. L., 1779	9.6	Located on eastern slope of Sleeping Ute Mountain. Ruins of great archaeological value, relic of prehistoric inhabitants.

a Estimated.   b From Mar. 2, 1889, until Aug. 3, 1918, classified as a National Park.   c Donated to the United States.

HISTORY

THE NATIONAL MILITARY AND OTHER PARKS ADMINISTERED BY THE WAR DEPARTMENT

[NUMBER, 7; TOTAL AREA, 22 SQUARE MILES; CHRONOLOGICALLY IN ORDER OF CREATION]

Name	Location	When established	Statute reference L	Area (acres)	Special characteristics
Chickamauga and Chattanooga	Georgia and Tennessee	Aug. 19, 1890	26 Stat. L., 333, 978	6,543	Beautiful natural park—Embraces battle fields of Chickamauga and Missionary Ridge and scenes of other conflicts of the Civil War fought in the vicinity of Chattanooga during 1863.
Antietam Battle Field	Maryland	Aug. 30, 1890	26 Stat. L., 401	50	Scene of one of the greatest battles of the Civil War.
Shiloh	Tennessee	Dec. 27, 1894	28 Stat. L., 597	3,546	Natural park embracing the battle field of Shiloh near Pittsburg Landing.
Gettysburg 1	Pennsylvania	Feb. 11, 1895	28 Stat. L., 651	2,451	Beautiful natural park—Scene of Civil War combat—Probably better marked than any other battle field in the world.
Vicksburg	Mississippi	Feb. 21, 1899	30 Stat. L., 841	1,323	Beautiful natural park—Scene of the siege and surrender of Vicksburg in 1863 during the Civil War.
Lincoln's Birthplace 1	Kentucky	July 17, 1916	39 Stat. L., 385	....	Contains the log cabin and part of the farm where Abraham Lincoln was born.
Guilford Courthouse	North Carolina	Mar. 2, 1917	39 Stat. L., 996	125	Near Greensboro—Scene of one of the great battles of the Revolution; fought in 1781.

1 Donated in whole or in part to the United States.

THE NATIONAL MONUMENTS ADMINISTERED BY THE WAR DEPARTMENT

[NUMBER, 2; TOTAL AREA, 6 ACRES; CHRONOLOGICALLY IN ORDER OF CREATION]

Name	Location	Date of creation	Statute reference of proclamation	Area (acres)	Special characteristics
Big Hole Battle Field 2	Montana	June 23, 1910	....	5	Site of battle field on which battle was fought Aug. 9, 1877, between a small force of United States troops and a much larger force of Nez Perce Indians, resulting in rout for the Indians.
Cabrillo (kä-brēl'yō)	California	Oct. 14, 1913	38 Stat. L., 1965	1	Of historic interest because of discovery of the territory now partly embraced in the State of California by Juan Rodriguez Cabrillo, who at this point first sighted land on Sept. 28, 1542.

1 Estimated   2 Set aside by Executive order.

THE NATIONAL MONUMENTS ADMINISTERED BY THE DEPARTMENT OF AGRICULTURE

[NUMBER, 10; TOTAL AREA, 509½ SQUARE MILES; CHRONOLOGICALLY IN ORDER OF CREATION]

Name	Location	Date of creation	Statute reference of proclamation	Area (acres)	Special characteristics
Gila Cliff Dwellings (ĭhē´lä)	New Mexico	Nov. 16, 1907	35 Stat. L., 2162	160	Numerous cliff-dweller ruins of much interest and in good preservation.
Tonto	Arizona	Dec. 19, 1907	35 Stat. L., 2168	1 640	Do.
Jewel Cave	South Dakota	Feb. 7, 1908	35 Stat. L., 2180	1 1,280	Limestone cavern of much beauty and considerable extent, limits of which are as yet unknown.
Wheeler	Colorado	Dec. 7, 1908	35 Stat. L., 2214	300	Of much interest from geological standpoint as example of eccentric erosion and extinct volcanic action. Of much scenic beauty.
Mount Olympus	Washington	Mar. 2, 1909 Apr. 17, 1912 May 11, 1915	35 Stat. L., 2247 37 Stat. L., 1737 39 Stat. L., 1726	608,640 608,480 299,370	Contains many objects of great and unusual scientific interest, including many glaciers. Is summer range and breeding ground of the Olympic elk.
Oregon Caves	Oregon	July 12, 1909	36 Stat. L., 2497	480	Extensive caves in limestone formation of much beauty; magnitude not entirely ascertained.
Devil Postpile	California	July 6, 1911	37 Stat. L., 1715	800	Spectacular mass of hexagonal basaltic columns, like an immense pile of posts. Said to rank with famous Giant's Causeway in Ireland.
Walnut Canyon	Arizona	Nov. 30, 1915	39 Stat. L., 1761	960	Contains cliff dwellings of much scientific and popular interest.
Bandelier (Bän-dĕ-lēr´)	New Mexico	Feb. 11, 1916	39 Stat. L., 1764	22,075	Vast number of cliff-dweller ruins, with artificial caves, stone sculpture, and other relics of prehistoric life.
Old Kasaan (kä-sän)	Alaska	Oct. 25, 1916	39 Stat. L., 1812	38.3	Abandoned Indian village in which there are numerous remarkable totem poles and other objects of historical interest.

1 Estimated

visitors to the parks numbered 69,018, as against 919,504 in 1920. Twelve of the national monuments were visited by 54,277 persons in 1919; by 138,951 the following year. These figures illustrate very graphically the steady increase in popular interest in the nation's playgrounds. A number of factors have contributed to this. A combination of the "See America First" movement and conditions of European travel brought about by the World War has caused more people to consider native resorts, in the planning of their vacations. The development of good roads and the automobile have played a part, as well as the great increase in recent years in the outdoor cult. Finally, the parks are better advertised than they used to be, not only by the Government but by private agencies which have discovered that advertising the parks in connection with their own business is not only good advertising from the standpoint of attractiveness but from that of increased returns as well. In addition to this, articles about the parks and their wonders have of late enjoyed a tremendous vogue in the popular magazines. The result of all this has been that hundreds of people are familiar with the parks to-day as compared with scores a few years ago. There is every reason to believe that this interest now solidly established will increase rather than diminish, that the parks will be visited by increasing throngs year by year; and that the visitors will be not alone from America but from other parts of the world as well, as a knowledge of what these priceless reservations contain becomes more widespread.

CHAPTER II

ACTIVITIES

In the preceding chapter the functions of the National Park Service—the supervision, management, and control of the various parks and monuments—have been pointed out; and some indication has necessarily been given of the activities of the Service in the performance of those functions. In considering the activities in detail it will simplify matters to go back for a moment to what may be termed the first principles of the Service, and note once more that the "National Park Idea," as expressed in the organic laws of the Service, the Yellowstone and the National Park Service acts, emphasizes two things: the retention of the parks, their scenery, natural wonders, forests, waters, etc., in their original state; and, the public enjoyment of the things and places thus conserved. The work of the National Park Service consists in the furtherance of these two objects, and all of its activities are concerned with either the conservation of the parks and monuments or the promotion of their use and enjoyment by the people. In discussing the Service's activities, therefore, attention will be given, first to conservational activities, and, then, to promotive activities.

Conservation of Physical Features. Conservational activities of the National Park Service are concerned with two kinds of conservation. First, there is the preservation in their natural states of the actual, physical parks themselves, their formations, their forests, and their waters. Then there is the protection of the wild life in the parks to the end that it may be preserved from extermination and given a chance to increase freely and develop in natural surroundings.

ACTIVITIES

Natural Wonders. The formations about the Yellowstone geysers and hot springs and rock and other formations in all the parks and monuments possess special attractions for the initial-cutting vandal and the souvenir-hunter. During the tourist season an important part of the work of the rangers consists in preventing depredations of this sort. Warning signs and printed regulations are also used. At the more important monuments, custodians are on duty, with a ranger or two in some instances to assist them in the summer months.

Ruins and Historic Structures. Before coming under Government protection many of the prehistoric cliff dwellings of the Southwest were being seriously injured by depredations of pottery and relic hunters and persons who, from sheer wantonness, injured and defaced the ruins. The ravages of time and the elements were also making inroads, and an unchecked deterioration was setting in. Most of these ruins and structures are located in monuments, though one important park, Mesa Verde, is chiefly notable because of the ruins it contains. The Service not only protects these places with resident custodians, printed warnings, and where possible, ranger patrol, but, as far as its funds will permit, performs considerable work of restoration. The Tumacacori Mission, for instance, a fine example of the Early Spanish mission architecture, is gradually being restored to its original condition. A rather novel expedient was adopted in the matter of the protection of Inscription Rock, in the El Morro Monument. This rock, which bears engraved upon its face many inscriptions of historic value, placed there by the early Spanish explorers, was becoming a target for the initial-carver, until a thick plantation of the spiny southwestern cactus and kindred plants was established around its base, creating an effectual *chevaux de frise* which renders the rock inaccessible without in any way interfering with its legitimate examination. An attempt is also being made, with the coöperation of the Bureau of Standards of the Department of Commerce, to cover the face of the rock with some transparent substance that will withstand the wear and tear of the elements.

The Service, with the coöperation of the Smithsonian Institution, also regulates the excavating and study of the ruins by legitimately interested persons and institutions. It also is gradually performing considerable work in excavation of the ruins along its own lines.

Forests and Plants. Protection of the forests and of the plant life of the parks constitutes one of the largest problems of the National Park Service, and a large part of the work of the ranger forces, especially during the dry months, which coincide with the tourist season and consequently with the season of camp fires, is directed toward this end. Fire is the greatest menace. It is guarded against by a strict supervision of camp fires, constant patrolling, frequently along strategically constructed fire trails, and observation from elevated stations connected by telephone with headquarters and with ranger stations. Close coöperation is maintained with the Forest Service in this connection, national forests adjoining most of the larger parks. The Service has long urged the appropriation of a large fund for use in fire emergencies, $100,000 being suggested to the Appropriations Committee by the Director at the 1920 hearings. In the act of March 4, 1921 (41 Stat. L., 1406) $25,000 was appropriated for that purpose, with the proviso that it be not used precautionarily and only after the expenditure has actually been incurred.

Live stock is a lesser menace to the forest and plant life, but the ranger forces exercise a strict supervision over the grazing of such herds as are permitted to enter any of the parks. All grazing is forbidden in the Yellowstone. Cattle, but not sheep, are allowed to graze in the other parks upon special permit from the Secretary of the Interior. Once in the parks they are kept by the ranger forces in certain designated areas.

Constant watchfulness is also maintained by the ranger and scientific forces to detect trees which have become infected with insect parasites, thus constituting a menace to the surrounding timber. The general policy is to remove no timber, but sometimes protection against the spread of parasitic infection renders such a course imperative. When this is done it must be in accordance with plans of the Landscape Engineer of the Service. Timber removed for use in the parks or because of maturity is removed under the same restrictions. Coöperation with the Bureau of Entomology of the Department of Agriculture is maintained in connection with protection against insect parasites.

Little difficulty is experienced in connection with wood stealing by campers and others. The practice, as well as the taking of wild flowers, is prohibited, and the regulation is enforced by the rangers.

Lakes and Streams. About the only direct activity of the Service in lake and stream conservation consists in the guarding against pollution of the waters. Water power in the parks is not utilized by private individuals, although the Service, in a number of instances, notably in the Yosemite, has erected power plants for the creation of light and power for its own use, and the use of some of its concessionaires. In coöperation with the Geological Survey some stream gaging is done, readings being taken by the park rangers.

Conservation of Wild Life. Hunting is not allowed in any of the parks,[1] and rigid restrictions are placed about the possession of fire-arms. The park rangers are continually on the lookout for poachers. Predatory animals, such as wolves, coyotes, and mountain lions are also hunted by the rangers, and efforts looking to their extermination are constantly going on. Many are trapped and sent away to zoos and menageries. Hard winters are the greatest menace to the game herds, however, especially in the Yellowstone, the country's greatest game preserve. In severe winters feeding of the elk, buffalo, and antelope becomes necessary. Hay is grown and cured

[1] Mount McKinley is an exception to the general rule. There, miners and prospectors are allowed to kill game to supply themselves with food. See Section 8 of act of February 26, 1917; 39 Stat. L., 938.

in the Yellowstone for winter feeding, the work being done on contract. Efforts are also made to keep the animals free from disease, coöperation being had with the Bureau of Animal Industry of the Agricultural Department for this purpose. An expert of this bureau vaccinates the tame buffalo herd of the Yellowstone each year. Close coöperation in the matter of game protection is maintained with the Bureau of Biological Survey, which maintains game preserves in Wind Cave and Sullys Hill parks, as well as in the Jacksons Hole country south of the Yellowstone. By virtue of an appropriation in the act of March 4, 1921 (41 Stat. L., 1407), the Service's activities in game protection have been extended to Mt. McKinley Park in Alaska. A minor activity of the Service in connection with wild life conservation is the distribution each year, particularly from the Yellowstone, of surplus animals from the elk, buffalo, and antelope herds. These animals are distributed either to other parks and monuments or to states and municipalities for placing in the local parks and zoölogical gardens.

All of the parks are bird refuges, and birds are protected from hunters and predatory animals while in the parks just as are the game herds. Many migratory birds find the parks safe stopping places each year on their passages back and forth between their breeding places in the north and their winter homes in the south.

Fishing with hook and line is permitted in the parks under regulations enforced by the park authorities, which regulations may be suspended by the Superintendent at any time and fishing absolutely prohibited in certain waters if in his judgment such action is advisable. The daily catch is limited, and a limit is also placed on the smallness of the fish to be taken. Coöperation is maintained with the Bureau of Fisheries, which maintains three hatcheries in Yellowstone Park and one in Glacier. There is also a state fish hatchery in Rocky Mountain Park; and a state hatchery which California has hitherto maintained in the Yosemite may be taken over by the Bureau of Fisheries. During the 1920 season 2,000,000 trout and grayling fry from the Yellowstone hatcheries were planted in the park waters. The Glacier hatchery planted 1,500,000 in Glacier Park.

Improvement. The Civil Engineering Section of the Service is charged with the planning of all road and trail extensions in the parks, as well as with the formulation of plans for all general engineering projects. Under the general supervision and control of this department the work of extending the roads and trails in the several parks is constantly going forward, depending upon the funds available for construction purposes.

The construction of bridges and culverts is also handled by this section, as are the preparation, and the equipment with conveniences, of camping and automobile parking sites. Other important activities of this section are the preparation of standard designs for such things as log bridges, timber and corrugated metal culverts of various sizes, and concrete arch culverts of standard widths. Standard specifications are also prepared for the purchasing of all sorts of construction equipment and miscellaneous supplies and tools. Drawings are prepared for standard ranger cabins and administrative buildings; plans and estimates of proposed work in different parks are reviewed, and engineering studies are made of the problems confronting the several parks in improvement matters.

In the prosecution of all its improvement activities the Service endeavors, through its Section of Landscape Engineering, to make each improvement undertaken blend harmoniously into a carefully considered scheme, in order to secure a maximum of beauty and convenience with a minimum of interference with natural conditions. This scheme is had in mind in the planning of vista cuttings, the removal of dead and down timber, the location of trails, roads, and bridges, and the location and construction of buildings for the administrative and coöperative units of the parks. It is an invariable rule that no structure of importance, whether for the Service or the public operators, can be erected until the approval of the Landscape Engineer has been secured, both as to location and design. The Landscape Engineering Section also devotes considerable attention to the removal of snags and dead timber from lakes and streams.

In a number of the parks the Service has established light and power plants, to supply both its own needs and those of the concessionaires, to whom light and power are sold at fixed rates. The most important of these plants was completed in the Yosemite in 1917 at a cost of $150,000. Water supply systems are also maintained by the Service at the principal parks, the water being piped to the free camping sites as well as to the buildings of the Service and the hotels of the public operators.

Sewer systems and sanitary control schemes are also maintained by the Service with the coöperation of the United States Public Health Service, which details experts to study the problems involved and to make recommendations.

The activities mentioned above are all direct activities. A large amount of improvement work has also been done in the parks indirectly, through the medium of public operators or concessionaires. The system of hotels established in Glacier Park by the Great Northern Railway has already been mentioned. The Yosemite National Park Company, composed of citizens of Los Angeles and San Francisco, is performing a similar work in the Yosemite. A Seattle-Tacoma syndicate is spending large sums in the creation of a hotel system in the Mt. Rainier Park. The policy of the Service with regard to concessions is to grant a monopoly of all principal service requirements, such as hotel service and transportation, to one responsible concern, retaining the right to supervise the rates charged. It has been found that the elimination of competition has given the public a better grade of service.

Rate supervision extends also to the regulation of charges for gasoline, groceries, oil, etc. The superintendents fre-

ACTIVITIES 57

quently check up the prices charged, and it is the belief of the Service that rates are reasonable, considering the distance of the parks from the regular centers of distribution.

In the Yosemite a system of parcel post delivery of groceries, etc., in the trucks of the Post Office Department, has been started, deliveries being made to campers every day. The plan has worked well, and it is proposed to extend it to other parks at an early date.

Maintenance. Service activities along the lines of maintenance involve such operations as the resurfacing of roads, the repairing of bridges and culverts, the painting and general repair of buildings, the keeping clean of trails, the overhauling and repair of equipment—in short, the maintaining of that constant vigilance against deterioration without which no enterprise can hope to remain "fit." A large part of the annual appropriations for the parks are on account of maintenance.

Protection Service. There is little disorder in the parks today, particularly in those in which national jurisdiction is complete. Persons rendering themselves obnoxious are warned, and removed from the park in which they happen to be if the warning does not suffice. If the offense is more serious they are arrested and brought before the United States Commissioner for trial or commitment. Every effort is made by the ranger forces to protect the law-abiding tourist from the carelessness or wantonness of the law-breaking element. For a camp fire left burning or garbage undisposed of, a party is liable to be brought back a distance of several miles to perform the unfulfilled duty. Traffic regulations are also enforced by the rangers in order to lessen the liability of accident by collision or otherwise. Sanitary regulations are enforced as a precaution against disease. Protection of tourists against exploitation through overcharging has already been mentioned.

An important indirect protective activity is the furnishing of medical service and hospital facilities to park vistors, park employees and their families, and concessionaires and their employees. There is no standardized plan with regard to the supplying of this service; but in general it may be said that the park surgeons are themselves concessionaires, giving a stipulated service in return for agreed-upon privileges. Thus, in the Yellowstone and Grand Canyon an arrangement has been made in coöperation with the U. S. Public Health Service, which pays the surgeon a fixed salary as its local representative. In addition the surgeon is allowed to practice in the park and to charge for his services according to a scale of prices fixed by the National Park Service. In the Yosemite, a surgeon is employed on a contract which calls for the supplying, by the surgeon, of medical services within certain prescribed limits to employees, concessionaires, etc. In return the surgeon is allowed to sell his services to tourists at a fixed rate, and, in addition, is paid a lump sum by the Service, the agreed amount being provided by deducting from the monthly salary of each employee an amount proportioned to his grade of pay. The Service possesses in the Yellowstone a hospital with facilities for 100 beds,—a legacy from the days of army administration.

Publicity. A detailed statement regarding the publications of the National Park Service will be found in the appendix. Their preparation and distribution are important promotive activities, their object being to spread a knowledge of the parks and the means of enjoying them among the people. For most of the parks there is now published each year an attractive booklet which contains, besides the rules and regulations and a number of attractive illustrations, information as to hotel rates, railways, etc. A number of good auto maps of several of the parks are also published. In this work there is cordial coöperation with the Geological Survey. The National Park Service also has for loaning purposes a number of pictures of the parks, as well as reels of motion pictures illustrating the wild life and scenery in the parks and monu-

ACTIVITIES

ments, thus complementing its activity of bringing the people to the parks by means of its informative literature. The Service's supply of such material is about worn out, and no provision is being made for its renewal. Further applications, therefore, are not being encouraged. Funds were provided originally through private donation.

CHAPTER III

ORGANIZATION

The organization of the National Park Service comprises five principal sections as follows:
- (a) Administration
- (b) The Field Service
- (c) The Editorial Section
- (d) The Law Section
- (e) The Publications Section

With the exception of the Field Service the above sections of the central organization are located in Washington, in the Interior Department Building, on the block bounded by E and F, 18th and 19th Streets, N.W.

Administration. The Director is responsible under the National Park Service act for the supervision, management, and control of the parks and monuments, subject to the general direction of the Secretary of the Interior. The office of the Director, therefore, is the apex of the Service's administration, exercising a general supervision over it and deciding all questions of policy arising which cannot be delegated and which are not of sufficient importance to be submitted to the Secretary of the Interior.

Two other offices are connected with the work of the administration,—the office of the Assistant Director and the office of the Chief Clerk.

The functions of the Assistant Director in matters of administration are twofold: to relieve the Director of matters of general administrative detail; and to act in the Director's stead during his absences in the field.

ORGANIZATION

Direct responsibility for routine matters of administration is centered in the office of the Chief Clerk. This office contains the followng units: Accounts, Stenographic, Personnel, Files, Messenger Service.

The Accounts Unit has charge of bookkeeping, property accountability, etc.; primarily with respect to the Service as a whole; secondarily as regards supervision of the accounts of the several parks and monuments.

The Personnel Unit deals with appointments, records of employees, etc. The duties of the other units are sufficiently described by their titles.

Field Service. The Field Service includes all of the National Park Service not permanently employed in the national capital. From this has developed the frequently employed arrangement of classifying the Park Service into two principal branches—the Service in the District of Columbia, and the Field Service. The latter comprises all those park superintendents, monument custodians, engineers, rangers and subordinate employees whose work lies away from Washington and directly in and with the parks and monuments themselves. In other words, they constitute the line of the National Park Service; the Washington organization, the staff. The organization of the Field Service in general is gone into in some detail in the paragraph below entitled "Individual Park Organization," and additional comment upon it is unnecessary, save in one particular. This has to do with the Civil Engineering and Landscape Engineering Sections, commonly referred to collectively as the Field Service At Large.

This most important part of the Field Service is referred to as "At Large" partly because its work lies everywhere throughout the system, not being confined to any park or section of the country; partly, and primarily, because of the method of its creation. No direct appropriations have ever been made for its personnel, and the fund for salaries is obtained by deducting a percentage from the various park appropriations for improvement and maintenance. This system was adopted in 1914 by the late Secretary Lane after securing a favorable opinion as to its legality from the Comptroller of the Treasury.[1]

Under the general supervision of the Director and Assistant Director the Field Service At Large is engaged in the various engineering activities carried on in the parks and monuments, which activities have been sufficiently described in the preceding chapter. As a general rule both the Civil and the Landscape Engineers make their headquarters in the parks wherein, for the time being, they are actively engaged. It sometimes happens, however, that one of them may be supervising projects in several parks at the same time; in which case a temporary headquarters may be established at some central point, equally convenient to all the places where work is going on. Thus, when one of them has work going on simultaneously in the California Parks, Crater Lake, Rainier and Yellowstone, he establishes an office in Portland, Oregon, and from there directs the work, going out to the several operations from time to time.

Editorial Section. The preparation of all Service publications, such as the annual reports, books of rules and regulations of the various parks and monuments, special bulletins, etc., is entrusted to the Editorial Section, subject to the general direction of the Director and Assistant Director. In addition to preparing the text of all publications, this section also prepares, through its drafting force, all maps, graphic charts, etc., to accompany publications and all blue prints, charts, etc., required by the Director for the general use of the Service. The section also edits all park publications, such as scientific monographs, etc., prepared elsewhere.

Law Section. The work of the Law Section of the Service covers a wide range. All legal questions arising within the organization are referred to it, as are similar questions pro-

[1] H. doc. 515 64 Cong., 1 sess., pp. 18-19.

ORGANIZATION 63

pounded to the Service by the park superintendents and field men. It prepares leases and contracts in connection with the working of the concessionaire system in the parks and passes upon similar documents submitted to the department. All of the title work in connection with lands presented to or purchased by the Government for park uses is likewise done by the Law Section. Besides the work mentioned above there are contracts for the construction of buildings and bridges to be drawn and let, all legal correspondence of a general nature to be handled, and advice to be given concessionaires as to what they can legally do in varying situations and states of fact. In addition this section keeps informed regarding all legislation affecting the parks and advises the Director in regard thereto.

Publications Section. As soon as a Service publication has been prepared for the printer the responsibility of the Editorial Section in connection with it ceases, and it passes into the jurisdiction of the Publications Section. This section has full charge of the distribution of the Service publications, answering all inquiries in regard thereto, keeping the mailing lists of the Service up to date, and, in general, performing all work pertaining to the Service's publications not of a preparatory or editorial nature.

Individual Park Organization—the Yellowstone. No standardized system of internal organization for the individual parks has as yet been adopted. In general features, however, park organization is similar to the general service organization. This is especially true of the larger parks, the most important of which, the Yellowstone, is organized under a superintendent and an assistant superintendent into ten sections which may be described as the sections of Administration, Information, Protection, Transportation, Light and Power, Communication, Sanitation, Painting, Machinery, and Engineering. This characterization is necessarily rough and does not in every case fully describe the work of the unit.

Administration. The general office management detail is about evenly divided between the Assistant Superintendent, who is in general charge, and the Chief Clerk. The former handles monthly and special reports, the collecting and recording of revenue, appointments, leaves of absence, and employees' compensation; he also has general supervision of the officers' mess and the headquarters labor mess, the telephone and telegraph office, the park files and records, the upkeep of offices and grounds, and the force of night watchmen and janitors.

The Chief Clerk has direct charge of the disbursement of funds, the recording of allotments, the purchase of supplies, the preparation of vouchers, cost accounting, and the preparation of inventories, pay rolls, and financial statements for the Superintendent. He also has charge of the collection and distribution of all park mail and receives all time reports and reports regarding material or supplies used and applied to specific work.

Information. The Park Naturalist is in charge of this section, and his duties, in addition to supervising the information service and museum, include the gathering of park specimens and data, the editing of park publications, the scientific inspection of forests for tree parasites and diseases, the supervision of wood cutting, the designation of trees to be cut for building purposes, the care of the park library and photographic files, and the handling of special assignments.

Protection. The Chief Ranger is the protector in chief of the park, and is charged with its general policing, all fire prevention and control, the protection of wild life, the destruction of predatory animals, the winter feeding of animals, the operation of buffalo and hay ranches, the control of grazing of milch cows and horses of concessionaires, the planting of fish, the keeping of records for the Weather Bureau, and the gaging of streams for the Geological Survey. He also has full control of all automobile traffic, including the registration of cars and the collection of fees.

ORGANIZATION 65

Transportation. The Steward and Master of Transportation is in charge of this unit, which has the custody and control of all motor equipment, except passenger cars assigned to park officers by the Superintendent; and all horses, horse equipment, forage, and supplies. All automobile and motor truck drivers and freighting teamsters are under this unit. Other duties with which it is charged include the care of all park property, except equipment, stationery, and supplies in the Superintendent's office; the operation and maintenance of the commissary and storehouse, and the control of the distribution in the park of all equipment and supplies.

Light and Power. This section, in charge of the Chief Electrician, maintains and operates power houses and power lines, looks after the lighting of buildings, and has control of all electrical equipment except telephone equipment and supplies.

Communication. The telephone and telegraph systems of the park are maintained and operated by this section under the supervision of the Chief Lineman. The Chief Lineman also inspects and reports upon the telephone and telegraph lines of public utilities and has custody of all telephone and telegraph equipment.

Sanitation. The Master Plumber is charged with all work in connection with sanitation and water supply. This includes the inspection of all sewer and water systems of hotels, camps and stores as well as the provision of sanitary and water supply systems for public automobile camps. The section is also charged with the custody and maintenance of fire-fighting equipment, sprinkling tank fixtures, and all plumbing and store supplies.

Painting. All painting of buildings, signs, automobiles, and equipment is done by this section under the Master Painter. The section also inspects the paint work of concessionaires and has custody of all park paint and glazing stores.

Machinery. The Master Mechanic, at the head of this section, has charge of all shops and machinery therein, and custody of all shop parts and supplies. General blacksmithing and horseshoeing and the upkeep and repair of automobiles, motorcycles, road machines, and fire-fighting equipment are in charge of this unit.

Engineering. The Park Engineer has charge of the construction, improvement, maintenance, and repair of all roads, bridges, and trails, and of all buildings, fences, formation walks, steps, and platforms except the fences of the buffalo and other ranches. He inspects contract work and the building operations of concessionaires. He gives technical advice to other park departments and makes technical investigations of park shops. He also has the custody and is charged with the upkeep of the park's files of plans, maps, charts and engineering data, and the surveying, drawing, and other engineering instruments.

APPENDIX 1

OUTLINE OF ORGANIZATION

Explanatory Note

The Outlines of Organization have for their purpose to make known in detail the organization and personnel possessed by the several services of the national government to which they relate. They have been prepared in accordance with the plan followed by the President's Commission on Economy and Efficiency in the preparation of its outlines of the organization of the United States Government.[1] They differ from those outlines, however, in that whereas the Commission's report showed only organization units, the presentation herein has been carried far enough to show the personnel embraced in each organization unit.

These outlines are of value not merely as an effective means of making known the organization of the several services. If kept revised to date by the services, they constitute exceedingly important tools of administration. They permit the directing personnel to see at a glance the organization and personnel at their disposition. They establish definitely the line of administrative authority and enable each employee to know his place in the system. They furnish the essential basis for making plans for determining costs by organization division and subdivision. They afford the data for a consideration of the problem of classifying and standardizing personnel and compensation. Collectively, they make it possible to determine the number and location of organization divisions of any particular kind, as, for example, laboratories, libraries,

[1] House Doc. 458, 62d. Congress, 2nd Session, 1912, 2 vols.

blue-print rooms, or any other kind of plant possessed by the national government, to what services they are attached and where they are located, or to determine what services are maintaining stations at any city or point in the United States. The Institute hopes that upon the completion of the present series, it will be able to prepare a complete classified statement of the technical and other facilities at the disposal of the government. The present monographs will then furnish the details regarding the organization, equipment, and work of the institutions so listed and classified.

OUTLINE OF ORGANIZATION

THE NATIONAL PARK SERVICE

DEPARTMENT OF THE INTERIOR

July 29, 1921

Organization Units; Classes of Employees	Number	Annual Salary Rate [1]
1. Washington Office		
1. Office of the Director		
Director	1	$4,500
Clerk	1	1,800
2. Office of the Assistant Director		
1. Office Proper of the Assistant Director		
Assistant Director	1	2,500
Clerk	1	1,800
2. Legal Section:		
Law Clerk	1	2,000
3. Editorial Section:		
Editor	1	2,000
Draftsman	1	1,800
4. Publication Section:		
Clerk	1	1,400
3. Office of the Chief Clerk		
1. Office Proper of the Chief Clerk		
Chief Clerk	1	2,000
Clerk	1	1,200
	1	1,020
	1	900
Messenger	1	600
2. Personnel Section:		
Clerk	1	1,600
3. Accounts Section:		
Accountant	1	1,800
Clerk	1	1,600
4. Files Section:		
Clerk	1	1,600

[1] Net, or without the temporary "bonus" or additional compensation of 60 per cent on classes below $400, of $240 on classes of $400 to $2500, and of an amount necessary to make the total compensation $2740 on classes of $2500 to $2740. This is subject to minor exceptions in special cases.

	1	900

2. Field Service
    Chief Civil Engineer — 1 — 4,000
    Landscape Engineer — 1 — 2,400 [a]
    Assistant Landscape Engineer — 1 — 2,000 [a]
    Assistant Engineer — 1 — 2,100
     — 1 (per month) — 200 [b]
     — 1 (per month) — 175 [b]
     — 1 (per month) — 175 [b]
    Office Engineer — 1 (per month) — 150
    General Foreman — 1 — 1,920
    Clerk-Stenographer — 1 — 1,400
     — 1 — 1,400 [c]

3. Parks and Monuments
    1. General Grant National Park, Kaweah, Calif.
        Acting Superintendent — 1 — ———
        Chief Park Ranger — 1 — 1,500
        Park Ranger — 1 (per month) — 85 [b]
         — 1 (per month) — 85 [c]
    2. Glacier National Park, Belton, Montana
        Superintendent — 1 — 3,000 [a]
        Clerk and Assistant Superintendent — 1 — 2,000 [a]
        Assistant Engineer — 1 — 2,400 [a]
        Clerk — 1 — 1,400 [a]
        Stenographer and Typist — 1 — 1,200
        Clerk-Stenographer — 3 (per month) — 100 [b]
        General and Mill Foreman — 1 — 1,400
        Teamster — 1 — 1,080
        Carpenter and Park Ranger — 1 (per month) — 105 [c]
        Chief Park Ranger — 1 — 1,500 [a]
        First Assistant Chief Park Ranger — 1 — 1,440
        Assistant Chief Park Ranger — 2 — 1,300
        Park Ranger — 6 — 1,200
         — 4 (per month) — 100 [b]
         — 2 (per month) — 100 [a]
         — 1 (per diem) — 1
    3. Grand Canyon National Park, Grand Canyon, Ariz.
        Superintendent — 1 — 3,000
        General Construction Foreman — 1 — 1,800
        Chief Park Ranger — 1 — 1,500
        Park Ranger — 1 — 1,200
        Stenographer and Typist — 1 — 1,600 [a]
        Park Ranger — 6 (per month) — 100
         — 1 — 1,200 [b]
        Stenographer and Typist — 1 — 1,020 [a]

[a] Quarters furnished.
[b] Temporary
[c] When actually employed.

OUTLINE OF ORGANIZATION

4. Hot Springs National Park, Arkansas
   - Superintendent — 1 — 3,600
   - Chief Clerk and Assistant to Superintendent — 1 — 1,600
   - Clerk-Stenographer — 1 — 1,200
   - Consulting Engineer — 1 — 12
   - Policeman — 2 — 1,300
   - — 4 — 1,000
   - Foreman — 1 — 1,500
   - Manager Free Bath house — 1 — 1,300
   - Head Male Attendant — 1 — 1,000
   - Attendant — 4 — 720
   - — 2 — 600
   - Laborer — 10 — 840
   - — 3 — 720

5. Lafayette National Park, Bar Harbor, Maine
   - Superintendent — 1 — 1,000
   - Clerk-Typist — 1 — 1,200
   - Stenographer and Typist — 1 — 1,200
   - Ornithologist — 1 — 1
   - Chief Park Ranger — 1 — 1,320
   - Park Ranger — 2 — 1,200
   - Botanist — 1 — 1

6. Mesa Verde National Park, Mancos, Colorado
   - Superintendent — 1 — 2,400
   - Park Ranger — 2 — 1,320
   - — 1 (per month) — 75

7. Rocky Mountain National Park, Estes Park, Colorado
   - Superintendent — 1 — 3,000
   - Clerk-Stenographer — 1 — 1,500
   - Clerk — 1 — 1,200
   - Park Ranger — 2 — 1,200
   - — 1 — 960
   - — 10 (per month) — 80 [b]
   - — 1 — 1,200 [b]

8. Sullys Hill National Park, Ft. Totten, N. D.
   - Acting Superintendent [2]

9. Platt National Park, Sulphur, Oklahoma
   - Superintendent — 1 — 1,500
   - Clerk — 1 — 1,200 [a]
   - Laborer — 1 — 780
   - — 1 — 720
   - — 1 — 480

[a] Quarters furnished.
[b] Temporary
[2] Supervised by the principal of the Indian School at Fort Totten, N. Dak., who serves without salary.

THE NATIONAL PARK SERVICE

Park Ranger	1	660

10. Crater Lake National Park, Medford, Oregon

Superintendent	1	2,000
Clerk-Typist	1	1,320
Park Ranger	6 (per month)	90 [b]

11. Yosemite National Park, Yosemite, Calif.

Superintendent	1	3,600
Assistant Superintendent	1	2,220 [a]
Park Supervisor	1	2,040 [a,c]
Assistant Park Supervisor	1	1,680 [c]
Engineer	1	2,400 [a]
Clerk	1	1,500 [a]
Storekeeper and Property Clerk	1	1,200
Stenographer and Typist	1	1,200 [a]
Clerk-Stenographer and Typist	1	1,200 [a]
Clerk	1	1,080 [c]
Clerk-Stenographer	1	1,080
Stenographer and Typist	1 (per month)	75
Forester	1	1,800
Master Mechanic	1	1,800 [c]
Power Station Operator	1	1,200
	1	1,200 [c]
	1 (per month)	100 [a]
Assistant Mechanic	1	1,360
General Blacksmith	1	1,200
General Painter	1	1,200
General Plumber	1	1,320 [c]
Chief Electrician	1	1,800
Electrician	1	1,320
Line Foreman	1	1,200 [c]
General Carpenter	1	1,320
Carpenter	1	1,200 [c]
Head Teamster	1	1,200
Skilled Laborer	1	1,140
Telephone Operator	2	720
	2 (per month)	60 [b]
	1	720 [b]
	2 (per diem)	2.40 [b]
Telegraph Operator	3 (per month)	100 [b]
Naturalist	1	1,500
Chief Park Ranger	1	1,800
Park Ranger	1	1,200
	1	1,350
	1	1,200
	4	1,200 [b]
	2 (per month)	100 [b]

[a] Quarters furnished.
[b] Temporary
[c] When actually employed.

APPENDICES

	1 (per month)	90 [b]
	7 (per month)	75 [b]
	1 (per month)	75 [c]
	1	1,200 [c]
12. Wind Cave National Park, Hot Springs, S. D.		
Superintendent	1	1,800 [a]
Park Ranger	1	1,080
	2 (per month)	100 [b]
13. Zion National Park, Springdale, Utah		
Chief Park Ranger and Acting Superintendent	1	1,300
Park Ranger	1	960
	1 (per month)	75 [b]
14. Mount Rainier National Park, Ashford, Washington		
Superintendent	1	3,000
Clerk	1	1,500
Warehouse Clerk	1 (per month)	90 [b]
Clerk-Telephone Operator	2 (per month)	70 [b]
Stenographer	1 (per month)	90 [b]
Chief Park Ranger	1	1,500
Park Ranger	1	1,200
	1 (per month)	90
	11 (per month)	90 [b]
15. Sequoia National Park, Kaweah, Calif.		
Superintendent	1	2,400 [a]
Clerk	1	1,400 [a]
Assistant Chief Park Ranger	1	1,500
	1	1,350
Chief Park Ranger	1	1,500
Park Ranger	1	1,100 [c]
	1	480
	1 (per month)	85 [a]
	2	900 [c]
	3 (per month)	75 [b]
	1 (per month)	85 [b c]
	1 (per month)	75 [b c]
16. Yellowstone National Park, Yellowstone, Wyoming		
Superintendent	1	4,000
Assistant Superintendent	1	2,500
Assistant Engineer	1	2,400 [a]
Surveyor	1 (per month)	150
	8	1,200 [a c]
	5	1,200 [c]

[a] Quarters furnished.
[b] Temporary
[c] When actually employed.

THE NATIONAL PARK SERVICE

Purchasing Clerk	1		2,100
Clerk	1		1,440
	1		1,320
	1	(per month)	110
Stenographer and Typist	1		1,320 [a]
	1		1,200 [a]
Stenographer	1	(per month)	100 [a]
Park Naturalist	1		1,500 [a]
Steward and Master of Transportation	1		1,680 [a]
Master Mechanic	1		1,680 [a]
Auto Mechanic	2	(per month)	120 [a]
Carpenter	2		1,320 [a]
Electrician	1		1,200 [a]
Assistant Electrician	1		1,200
Chief Lineman	1		1,500
Watchman	1	(per month)	90 [a][b]
Blacksmith	1		1,320 [a]
Master Painter	1		1,500 [a]
Master Plumber	1		1,500 [a]
Foreman	2		1,800 [a]
	2		1,680 [a]
	1		1,560 [a]
	1		1,320 [a]
Telegraph Operator	1		1,200
Telephone Switchboard Operator	2	(per hour)	.35 [b][c]
	1		900
Chief Buffalo Keeper	1		1,500 [a]
Assistant Chief Buffalo Keeper	1		1,200
	1		1,200 [a]
Buffalo Herder	1		75 [a][b]
Handyman	1		1,200 [a]
Laborer	3		1,080 [a]
Chief Ranger	1		1,620
First Assistant Chief Park Ranger	1		1,500 [a]
Assistant Chief Park Ranger	1		1,440
	1		1,320 [a]
Park Ranger	4		1,200 [a]
	6		1,200
	8		1,200 [a][c]
	5		1,200 [c]
	3		1,320 [a]
	1		1,320 [a][b]
	12	(per month)	100 [a][c]
	26	(per month)	80 [a]

17. Casa Grande National Monument, Blackwater, Ariz.

Custodian	1		1,320

[a] Quarters furnished.
[b] Temporary.
[c] When actually employed.

OUTLINE OF ORGANIZATION

18. Montezuma Castle National Monument,
    Camp Verde, Ariz.
    Custodian   1   12
19. Navajo National Monument, Kayenta,
    Ariz.
    Custodian   1   12
20. Papago Saguaro National Monument,
    Tempe, Ariz.
    Custodian   1   12
21. Petrified Forest National Monument,
    Adamana, Ariz.
    Custodian   1   12
22. Tumacacori National Monument,
    Blackwater, Ariz.
    Custodian   1   12
23. Muir Woods National Monument, Calif.
    Custodian   1   12
24. Colorado National Monument, Grand
    Junction, Colo.
    Custodian   1   12
25. Sitka National Monument, Alaska
    Custodian   1   12
26. Scotts Bluff National Monument,
    Gering, Nebraska
    Custodian   1   12
27. Capulin Mountain National Monument,
    Folsom, N. Mex.
    Custodian   1   12
28. El Morro National Monument, Ramah,
    N. Mex.
    Custodian   1   12
29. Verendrye National Monument, Sanish,
    N. Dak.
    Custodian   1   12
30. Devils Tower National Monument,
    Hulett, Wyoming
    Custodian   1   12

ᵃ Quarters furnished.
ᶜ Temporary.

Note.—No showing is made above for Lassen, Hawaii, or Mt. McKinley National Parks, the reason being that lack of appropriations has until recently made it impracticable for the Service to employ a regular staff for the guardianship of these areas. Under the 1922 appropriations, however, it will be possible to take this step in the cases of Hawaii and Mt. McKinley. The former will be looked after by a superintendent, a clerical assistant, and two rangers. A ranger and an assistant will take care of Mt. McKinley. Lassen, as heretofore, will be guarded by the forest rangers from the neighboring Lassen National Forest.

APPENDIX 2

CLASSIFICATION OF ACTIVITIES

Explanatory Note

The classifications of activities have for their purpose to list and classify in all practicable detail the specific activities engaged in by the several services of the national government. Such statements are of value from a number of standpoints. They furnish, in the first place, the most effective showing that can be made in brief compass of the character of work performed by the service to which they relate. Secondly, they lay the basis for a system of accounting and reporting that will permit the showing of total expenditures classified according to activities. Finally, taken collectively, they make possible the preparation of a general or consolidated statement of the activities of the government as a whole. Such a statement will reveal in detail, not only what the government is doing, but the services in which the work is being performed. For example, one class of activities that would probably appear in such a classification is that of "scientific research." A subhead under this class would be "chemical research." Under this head would appear the specific lines of investigation under way and the services in which they were being prosecuted. It is hardly necessary to point out the value of such information in planning for future work and in considering the problem of the better distribution and coördination of the work of the government. The Institute contemplates attempting such a general listing and classification of the activities of the government upon the completion of the present series.

Classification Of Activities

1. Conservation
    1. Natural Wonders
    2. Prehistoric Structures
    3. Historic Ruins and Structures
    4. Forests and Plant Life
    5. Lakes and Streams
    6. Scenic Effects
    7. Animals
    8. Birds
    9. Fish
2. Construction and Maintenance
    1. Roads
    2. Trails
    3. Bridges
    4. Vistas
    5. Camping Grounds
    6. Administrative Buildings
3. Protection
    1. Sanitation
    2. Policing
    3. Accident Prevention
4. Compilation of Statistics
    1. Stream Flow
    2. Weather Records
    3. Use of Parks
    4. Animal Increase
5. Scientific Research
    1. Tree Inspection
    2. Specimen Collecting
    3. Animal and Bird Study
    4. Archæology

APPENDIX 3

PUBLICATIONS

The National Park Service publishes, (1) historic and scientific pamphlets; (2) rules and regulations; (3) maps and manuals; (4) panoramic views; (5) reports and proceedings. A complete list of these publications, together with all necessary information as to how they may be procured, may be found in the annual report of the Director.

Historic and Scientific Pamphlets. These publications, of which there are twenty-six in all published, range in size from twelve to 260 pages. Three of them are free. The others cost from five cents to one dollar, depending upon the size and elaborateness of the publication.

Rules and Regulations. These booklets, attractively prepared, with illustrations and maps, have been published for fourteen of the parks, including all of the most important ones. For three of the remaining parks they have been got out in mimeographed form without illustration. Besides the rules and regulations, they contain a great deal of valuable information regarding hotels, points of interest, etc. These publications are all free.

Maps and Manuals. Besides a general map showing all the parks and monuments administered by the Service, automobile road and trail maps are published for the eight most important parks. A handy manual for motorists, in small pamphlet form, is also published containing the most important features of the Rules and Regulations and special information and advice for motorists. The maps and manuals are free.

Panoramic Views. These have been prepared for seven

PUBLICATIONS

of the parks and are sold at twenty-five cents a copy. They are based on accurate surveys and average in size about 18 x 20 inches, the scale being from one to three miles to the inch. They are printed in four colors.

Reports and Proceedings. The annual report of the Director does not differ essentially from that of the ordinary executive. It is a complete summary of the work of the Service during the fiscal year. It is free. At present the reports for 1918, 1919, 1920, and 1921 are available for distribution. The Proceedings of the four National Park Conferences are on sale at from fifteen cents to twenty-five cents a volume.

APPENDIX 4

LAWS

(A) INDEX TO LAWS

Administration, etc.	
Of monuments, appropriations for	41 Stat. L., 1406
Of parks, appropriations for	41 Stat. L., 1406
American Antiquities	
Punishment for destruction of	34 Stat. L., 225
Animals	
May be destroyed when	39 Stat. L., 535
Appropriations	
Administration, protection, maintenance, and improvement of parks	41 Stat. L., 1406
Administration, protection, maintenance, preservation, and improvement of monuments	41 Stat. L., 1406
Blackfeet Reservation Road, repairs to	41 Stat. L., 1406
Bridges and Culverts, Yellowstone	41 Stat. L., 1406
Buffalo in Yellowstone, care of	41 Stat. L., 1406
Community Centers, Yellowstone	41 Stat. L., 1406
El Portal Road, construction of	41 Stat. L., 1406
Federal Power Commission, limitations on use of	41 Stat. L., 1380
Fighting Forest Fires	41 Stat. L., 1406
Fire Lookout Station, Yellowstone	41 Stat. L., 1406
Forest fires—not to be used precautionarily	41 Stat. L., 1406
Forest fires—to be allotted by Secretary of the Interior	41 Stat. L., 1406
Motor-driven vehicles—maintenance, etc., of	41 Stat. L., 1406
National Park Service in the District of Columbia	41 Stat. L., 1406
Ranger Stations, Yellowstone and Rainier	41 Stat. L., 1406
Replacement of Burned Buildings	41 Stat. L., 1406
Rest House, Yellowstone	41 Stat. L., 1406
Rights of Way in Grand Canyon—acquisition of	41 Stat. L., 1406
Roads in Glacier	41 Stat. L., 1406
Roads in Yellowstone	41 Stat. L., 1406
Roads in Yosemite	41 Stat. L., 1406
Salaries of Officers	39 Stat. L., 535
	40 Stat. L., 20
	41 Stat. L., 1406

[1] This index refers to the general laws—Special acts affecting individual parks are referred to in the general index to this volume.

LAWS

Shelter Cabin, Rainier	41 Stat. L., 1406
Snow Removal in Yellowstone, limitation on expenditure for	41 Stat. L., 1406
Toll Roads in Grand Canyon, expenditures for forbidden	41 Stat. L., 1406
Arrest	
Authority of Officer to	33 Stat. L., 700
Without Process—when permissible	33 Stat. L., 700
Blackfeet Indian Reservation, appropriation for road repair in	41 Stat. L., 1406
Bridges and Culverts	
In Yellowstone, appropriation for	41 Stat. L., 1406
Buffaloes	
In Yellowstone, appropriation for care of	41 Stat. L., 1406
Buildings	
Replacement of burned	41 Stat. L., 1406
Limitation on cost of	37 Stat. L., 460
Limitation on cost increased	40 Stat. L., 677
Coöperation	
With Secretary of Agriculture	39 Stat. L., 535
Creation	
National Park Service established	39 Stat. L., 535
Community Centers	
In Yellowstone, appropriation for	41 Stat. L., 1406
Donations	
Of lands, etc.,—Secretary of the Interior may accept	41 Stat. L., 917
Forest Fires	
Appropriation for lookout stations in Yellowstone	41 Stat. L., 1406
Appropriations for, not to be used precautionarily	41 Stat. L., 1406
Appropriations for, to be allotted by Secretary of the Interior	41 Stat. L., 1406
Penalties for setting, etc., provided	35 Stat. L., 1098
Secretary of the Interior to submit report on	41 Stat. L., 1406
Federal Power Commission	
May not license power development in parks	41 Stat. L., 1353
Limitation on use of appropriation	41 Stat. L., 1380
Laws	
Codification of penal	35 Stat. L., 1098
Violations of relating to parks, arrests for	33 Stat. L., 700
Live Stock	
May not be grazed in Yellowstone	39 Stat. L., 535
Miners and Homesteaders	
Wood rights on public lands reserved	35 Stat. L., 1098
Monuments	
Contiguous to national forests, supervision of	39 Stat. L., 535
Creation of	34 Stat. L., 225
Excavation, etc., on, permits for	34 Stat. L., 225
Secretaries of Agriculture, Interior, and War to make rules to govern	34 Stat. L., 225

82   THE NATIONAL PARK SERVICE

Motor Vehicles	
Limitations on expenditures for	41 Stat. L., 1406
Natural Curiosities	
Free access to not to be interfered with	39 Stat. L., 535
Personnel	
Authority of, to arrest	33 Stat. L., 700
Duties of—in general	39 Stat. L., 535
Director	
How appointed	39 Stat. L., 535
Duties of	39 Stat. L., 535
Salary of	39 Stat. L., 535
	40 Stat. L., 20
	41 Stat. L., 1406
Assistant Director	
How appointed	39 Stat. L., 535
Salary of	39 Stat. L., 535
	40 Stat. L., 20
	41 Stat. L., 1406
Accountant—salary of	41 Stat. L., 1406
Chief Clerk	
How appointed	39 Stat. L., 535
Salary of	39 Stat. L., 535
	40 Stat. L., 20
	41 Stat. L., 1406
Clerks—salaries of	40 Stat. L., 20
	41 Stat. L., 1406
Draftsman—salary of	39 Stat. L., 535
	40 Stat. L., 20
	41 Stat. L., 1406
Editor—salary of	41 Stat. L., 1406
Employees appointed by Secretary of the Interior	39 Stat. L., 535
Experts, etc.,—limitation on employment of	39 Stat. L., 535
Law Clerk—salary of	41 Stat. L., 1406
Messenger	
How appointed	39 Stat. L., 535
Salary of	39 Stat. L., 535
	40 Stat. L., 20
	41 Stat. L., 1406
Superintendent of National Parks	
Authorization for employment of	39 Stat. L., 309
Appropriation for salary of	39 Stat. L., 23
Plant Life	40 Stat. L., 20
May be destroyed, when	39 Stat. L., 535
President of the United States may reserve monuments by proclamation	34 Stat. L., 225
Privileges	
In Grand Canyon to highest bidder	40 Stat. L., 1177
Limitations upon granting of	39 Stat. L., 535
Secretary of the Interior may grant discretionarily	39 Stat. L., 535

LAWS 83

Ranger Stations
  Appropriations for   41 Stat. L., 1406
Receipts and Expenditures
  Secretary of the Interior to submit statement of 36 Stat. L., 1421
Rest House
  Appropriation for   41 Stat. L., 1406
Revenues
  To be covered into Treasury   40 Stat. L., 153
Rights of Way
  Act relating to through parks, etc., not to be affected   39 Stat. L., 535
  Acquisition of for roads and trails in Grand Canyon   41 Stat. L., 1406
Roads
  In Glacier—appropriation for   41 Stat. L., 1406
  In Yellowstone—appropriation for   41 Stat. L., 1406
  In Yosemite—appropriation for   41 Stat. L., 1406
Rules and Regulations
  Arrest for violation of   33 Stat. L., 700
  Punishment for violation of   39 Stat. L., 535
  Secretaries of Agriculture, Interior, and War to make   34 Stat. L., 225
Secretary of Agriculture
  May permit excavation, etc., of antiquities   34 Stat. L., 225
  Shall coöperate in making rules and regulations for monuments   34 Stat. L., 225
  Shall coöperate with National Park Service, when 39 Stat. L., 535
Secretary of the Interior
  May accept donations for park purposes   41 Stat. L., 917
  May accept relinquishments of monument tracts 34 Stat. L., 225
  May destroy animals and plant life, when   39 Stat. L., 535
  May grant grazing permits   39 Stat. L., 535
  May grant privileges, leases, and permits   39 Stat. L., 535
  May permit excavation, etc., of antiquities   34 Stat. L., 225
  May sell timber, when   39 Stat. L., 535
  Shall allot forest fire funds   41 Stat. L., 1406
  Shall coöperate in making rules and regulations for monuments   34 Stat. L., 225
  Shall direct expenditures of Yellowstone appropriation   41 Stat. L., 1406
  Shall make rules and regulations   39 Stat. L., 535
  Shall submit estimates   40 Stat. L., 153
  Shall submit reports on forest fires   41 Stat. L., 1406
Secretary of War
  May permit excavations, etc., of antiquities   34 Stat. L., 225
  Shall coöperate in making rules and regulations for monuments   34 Stat. L., 225
Shelter Cabins
  Appropriation for   41 Stat. L., 1406
Snow
  In Yellowstone—removal of   41 Stat. L., 1406

84   THE NATIONAL PARK SERVICE

Toll Roads	
Expenditures on forbidden	41 Stat. L., 1406
United States Commissioners	
Shall issue process, when	33 Stat. L., 700
Water Power	
Development of in parks and monuments forbidden	41 Stat. L., 1353
Yellowstone	
Grazing forbidden in	39 Stat. L., 535

(B) Compilation Of Laws

General

1905—Act of February 6, 1905 (33 Stat. L., 700)—An Act For the protection of the public forest reserves and national parks of the United States.

That all persons employed in the forest-reserve and national-park service of the United States shall have authority to make arrests for the violation of the laws and regulations relating to the forest reserves and national parks, and any person so arrested shall be taken before the nearest United States Commissioner, within whose jurisdiction the reservation or national park is located, for trial; and upon sworn information by any competent person any United States Commissioner in the proper jurisdiction shall issue process for the arrest of any person charged with the violation of said laws and regulations; but nothing herein contained shall be construed as preventing the arrest by any officer of the United States, without process, of any person taken in the act of violating said laws and regulations.

1906—Act of June 8, 1906 (34 Stat. L., 225)—An Act For the preservation of American antiquities.

[Sec. 1]. That any person who shall appropriate, excavate, injure, or destroy any historic or prehistoric ruin or monument, or any object of antiquity, situated on lands owned or controlled by the Government of the United States, without the permission of the Secretary of the department of the Government having jurisdiction over the lands on which said antiquities are situated, shall, upon conviction, be fined in a sum of not more than $500 or be imprisoned for a period of not more than ninety days, or shall suffer both fine and imprisonment, in the discretion of the court.

Sec. 2. That the President of the United States is hereby authorized, in his discretion, to declare by public proclamation historic landmarks, historic and prehistoric structures, and other objects of historic or scientific interest that are situated upon the lands owned or controlled by the Government of the United States to be national monuments, and may reserve as a part thereof parcels of land, the limits of which in all cases shall be confined to the smallest area compatible with the proper care and management of the objects to be protected: *Provided,* That when such objects are situated upon a tract covered by a bona fide unperfected claim or held in private ownership, the tract, or so much thereof as may be necessary for the proper care and management of the object, may be relinquished to the Government, and the Secretary of the Interior is hereby authorized to accept the relinquishment of such tracts in behalf of the Government of the United States.

SEC. 3. That permits for the examination of ruins, the excavation of archæological sites, and the gathering of objects of antiquity upon the lands under their respective jurisdictions may be granted by the Secretaries of the Interior, Agriculture, and War to institutions which they may deem properly qualified to conduct such examination, excavation, or gathering, subject to such rules and regulations as they may prescribe: *Provided,* That the examinations, excavations, and gatherings are undertaken for the benefit of reputable museums, universities, colleges, or other recognized scientific or educational institutions, with a view to increasing the knowledge of such objects, and that the gatherings shall be made for permanent preservation in public museums.

SEC. 4. That the Secretaries of the departments aforesaid shall make and publish from time to time uniform rules and regulations for the purpose of carrying out the provisions of this act.[1]

1909—Act of March 4, 1909 (35 Stat. L., 1088, 1098)—An Act To codify, revise, and amend the penal laws of the United States.

Sections 49–53 inclusive, and 56, 57, and 60, provide penalties for timber depredations on public lands, reservations or Indian lands, reserving the usual wood rights of mining men and homesteaders; also for boxing trees for turpentine on public lands, or setting fires, failing to extinguish fires, breaking fences, driving cattle, and injuring survey marks and telegraph lines thereon.

1911—Act of March 4, 1911 (36 Stat. L., 1363, 1421)—An Act Making appropriations for sundry civil expenses of the Government for the fiscal year ending June thirtieth, nineteen hundred and twelve, and for other purposes.

* * * *

Hereafter the Secretary of the Interior shall submit in the annual

[1] Under authority of the foregoing act the various proclamations have been made establishing the national monuments. A list of these proclamations will be found under the section entitled "The National Monuments," Chapter I, supra.

Book of Estimates, following the estimates for each of the national parks, a classified statement of the receipts and expenditures for the complete fiscal year next preceding the fiscal year for which estimates of appropriations are submitted.

1912—Act of August 24, 1912 (37 Stat. L., 417, 460)—An Act Making appropriations for sundry civil expenses of the Government for the fiscal year ending June thirtieth, nineteen hundred and thirteen, and for other purposes.

* * * *

No expenditure for construction of administration or other buildings cost in case of any building exceeding one thousand dollars shall hereafter be made in any national park except under express authority of Congress: *Provided,* That this shall not apply to buildings now in the process of actual construction.

1916—Act of February 28, 1916 (39 Stat. L., 14, 23)—An Act Making appropriations to supply further urgent deficiencies in appropriations for the fiscal year ending June thirtieth, nineteen hundred and sixteen, and prior years, and for other purposes.

* * * *

There is appropriated, for the remainder of the fiscal year nineteen hundred and sixteen, from the several appropriations for protection, improvement, and management, and so forth, of the various national parks, including the Hot Springs Reservation, as well as from the revenues from privileges, and so forth, in the national parks and the Hot Springs Reservation, such sum or sums as the Secretary of the Interior in his judgment may deem necessary, to be expended in employment of the superintendent of national parks in the District of Columbia and in the field, and other necessary expenses in connection with the administration of the national parks and the Hot Springs Reservation; a detailed statement of such expenditures to be submitted to Congress.

1916—Act of July 1, 1916 (39 Stat. L., 262, 309)—An Act Making appropriations for sundry civil expenses of the Government for the fiscal year ending June thirtieth, nineteen hundred and seventeen, and for other purposes.

* * * *

The Secretary of the Interior is authorized to employ in the District of Columbia and elsewhere, and pay, during the fiscal year nineteen hundred and seventeen, out of the several appropriations for protection, improvement and management of the various national parks including the Hot Springs Reservation and out of the revenues from rentals and privileges derived therefrom, a superintendent of national parks and to assist him such clerical or other services, not exceeding four persons, as the Secretary shall determine, and also to pay from said funds all necessary expenses of subsistence and travel of said superintendent when absent on duty outside of the District of Columbia. A detailed statement of all expenditures hereunder shall be made to Congress at its next session.

1916—Act of August 25, 1916 (39 Stat. L., 535)—An Act To establish a National Park Service and for other purposes (as amended by act of June 2, 1920; 41 Stat. L., 732—An Act To Accept the cession by the State of California of exclusive jurisdiction of the lands embraced within the Yosemite National Park, Sequoia National Park, and General Grant National Park, respectively and for other purposes)

[SEC. 1]. That there is hereby created in the Department of the Interior a service to be called the National Park Service, which shall be under the charge of a director, who shall be appointed by the Secretary and who shall receive a salary of $4,500 per annum. There shall also be appointed by the Secretary the following assistants and other employees at the salaries designated: One assistant director, at $2,500 per annum; one chief clerk, at $2,000 per annum; one draftsman, at $1,800 per annum; one messenger, at $600 per annum; and, in addition thereto, such other employees as the Secretary of the Interior shall deem necessary: *Provided,* That not more than $8,100 annually shall be expended for salaries of experts, assistants, and employees within the District of Columbia not herein specifically enumerated unless previously authorized by law. The service thus established shall promote and regulate the use of the Federal areas known as national parks, monuments, and reservations hereinafter specified by such means and measures as conform to the fundamental purposes of the said parks, monuments, and reservations, which purpose is to conserve the scenery and the natural and historic objects and the wild life therein and to provide for the enjoyment of the same in such manner and by such means as will leave them unimpaired for the enjoyment of future generations.

SEC. 2. That the director shall, under the direction of the Secretary of the Interior, have the supervision, management, and control of the several national parks and national monuments which are now under the jurisdiction of the Department of the Interior, and of the Hot Springs Reservation in the State of Arkansas, and of such other national parks and reservations of like character as may be hereafter created by Congress: *Provided,* That in the supervision, management, and control of national monuments contiguous to national forests the Secretary of Agriculture may coöperate with said National Park Service to such extent as may be requested by the Secretary of the Interior.

SEC. 3. That the Secretary of the Interior shall make and publish such rules and regulations as he may deem necessary or proper for the use and management of the parks, monuments, and reservations under the jurisdiction of the National Park Service, *and any violations of any of the rules and regulations authorized by this act shall be punished by a fine of not more than $500, or imprisonment for not exceeding six months, or both, and be adjudged to pay all cost of the proceedings.*[1] He may also, upon terms and conditions to be fixed by him, sell or dispose of timber in those cases where in his judgment the cutting of such timber is required in order to control the attacks of insects or diseases or otherwise conserve the scenery or the natural or historic objects in any such park, monument, or reservation He may also provide in his discretion for the destruction of such animals and of such plant life as may be detrimental to the use of any of said parks, monuments, or reservations. He may also grant privileges, leases, and permits for the use of land for the accommodation of visitors in the various parks, monuments, or other reservations herein provided for, but for periods not exceeding twenty years;[2] and no natural curiosities, wonders, or objects of interest shall be leased, rented, or granted to any one on such terms as to interfere with free access to them by the public; *Provided, however,* That the Secretary of the Interior may, under such rules and regulations and on such terms as he may prescribe, grant the privilege to graze live stock within any national park, monument, or reservation herein referred to when in his judgment such use is not detrimental to the primary purpose for which such park, monument, or reservation was created, except that this provision shall not apply to the Yellowstone National Park.

SEC. 4. That nothing in this Act contained shall affect or modify the provisions of the act approved February fifteenth, nineteen hundred and one, entitled "An Act relating to rights of way through certain parks, reservations, and other public lands."

1917—Act of April 17, 1917 (40 Stat. L., 2, 20)—An Act Making appropriations to supply deficiencies in appropriations for the fiscal year ending June thirtieth, nineteen hundred and seventeen and prior fiscal years, and for other purposes.

* * * *

For employees from April fifteenth to June thirtieth, nineteen

[1] As amended.
[2] This clause does not fully apply to Grand Canyon Park. See proviso in Act of February 26, 1919; 40 Stat. L., 1177.

hundred and seventeen, inclusive, at annual rates of compensation as follows: Director, $4,500; assistant director, $2,500; chief clerk, $2,000; draftsman, $1,800; clerks—one of class three, two of class two, two at $900 each; messenger, $600; in all, for park service in the District of Columbia, $3,666.67, or so much thereof as may be necessary, to be in lieu of salaries, during such period, of the Superintendent of National Parks and four other persons authorized to be employed in the District of Columbia during the fiscal year nineteen hundred and seventeen by the sundry civil appropriation act approved July first, nineteen hundred and sixteen.

1917—Act of June 12, 1917 (40 Stat. L., 105, 153)—An Act Making appropriations for sundry civil expenses of the Government for the fiscal year ending June thirtieth, nineteen hundred and eighteen, and for other purposes.

* * * *

From and after July first, nineteen hundred and eighteen, all revenues of the national parks, except Hot Springs Reservation, Arkansas, shall be covered into the Treasury to the credit of miscellaneous receipts; and the Secretary of the Interior is directed to submit, for the fiscal year nineteen hundred and nineteen and annually thereafter, estimates of the amounts required for the care, maintenance, and development of the said parks.

1918—Act of July 1, 1918 (40 Stat. L., 634, 677)—An Act Making appropriations for sundry civil expenses of the Government for the fiscal year ending June thirtieth, nineteen hundred and nineteen, and for other purposes.

* * * *

The limitation of cost upon the construction of any administration or other building in any national park without express authority of Congress, contained in the sundry civil appropriation Act approved August twenty-fourth, nineteen hundred and twelve, is increased from $1,000 to $1,500.

1920—Act of June 5, 1920 (41 Stat. L., 874, 917)—An Act Making appropriations for sundry civil expenses of the Government for the fiscal year ending June thirtieth, nineteen hundred and twenty-one, and for other purposes.

* * * *

Hereafter the Secretary of the Interior in his administration of the National Park Service is authorized, in his discretion, to accept patented lands, rights of way over patented lands or other lands, buildings, or other property within the various national parks and national monuments, and moneys which may be donated for the purposes of the national park and monument system.

1921—Act of March 3, 1921 (41 Stat. L., 1353)—An Act To amend an act entitled "An Act To create a Federal Power Commission; to provide for the improvment of navigation; the development of water power; the use of the public lands in relation thereto; and to repeal section 18 of the River and Harbor Appropriation Act, approved August 8, 1917, and for other purposes," approved June 10, 1920.

That hereafter no permit, license, lease, or authorization for dams, conduits, reservoirs, power houses, transmission lines, or other works for storage or carriage of water, or for the development, transmission, or utilization of power, within the limits as now constituted of any national park or national monument shall be granted or made without specific authority of Congress, and so much of the act of Congress approved June 10, 1920, entitled "An Act to create a Federal Power Commission; to provide for the improvement of navigation; the development of water power; the use of the public lands in relation thereto; and to repeal section 18 of the River and Harbor Appropriation Act, approved August 8, 1917, and for other purposes," approved June 10, 1920, as authorizes licensing such uses of existing national parks and national monuments by the Federal Power Commission is hereby repealed.

1921—Act of March 4, 1921 (41 Stat. L., 1367, 1380, 1406)—An Act Making appropriations for sundry civil expenses of the Government for the fiscal year ending June 30, 1922, and for other purposes.

* * * *

That no portion of this appropriation [For . . . the Federal Power Commission . . . $100,000] shall be available for any expense connected with the leasing of any water-power facilities in any national park and national monument.

* * * *

National Park Service: Director, $4,500; assistant director, $2,500; chief clerk, $2,000; law clerk $2,000; editor, $2,000; draftsman, $1,800; accountant, $1,800; clerks—two of class four, three of class three (one transferred from Secretary's office), one of class two, one of class one, one $1,020, two at $900 each; messenger, $600; in all, for park service in the District of Columbia, $31,020.

Fighting forest fires in national parks: For fighting forest fires in national parks, or other areas administered by the National Park Service, or fires that endanger such areas, and for replacing buildings or other physical improvements that have been destroyed by forest fires within such areas, $25,000: *Provided,* That these funds shall not be used for any precautionary fire protection or patrol work prior to actual occurrence of the fire: *And provided further,* That the allotment of these funds to the various national parks, or areas administered by the National Park Service, for fire fighting purposes, shall be made by the Secretary of the Interior, and then only after the obligation for the expenditure has been incurred, and the Secretary of the Interior shall submit with his annual estimate of expenditures a report showing the location, size, and description of each forest fire, together with the number of men, their classification and rate of pay and actual time employed, and a statement of expenditures showing the cost for labor, supplies, special services, and other expenses covered by the expenditures made from these funds.

Crater Lake National Park, Oregon: For administration, protection, maintenance, and improvement, including not exceeding $600 for the maintenance, operation, and repair of a motor-driven passenger-carrying vehicle for the use of the superintendent and employees in connection with general park work, $25,300.

General Grant National Park, California: For adminstration, protection, maintenance, and improvement, $6,000.

Glacier National Park, Montana: For administration, protection, maintenance, and improvement, including necessary repairs to the roads from Glacier Park Station through the Blackfeet Indian Reservation to various points in the boundary line of the Glacier National Park and to the International Boundary, including not exceeding $2,400 for the maintenance, repair, and operation of motor-driven and horse-drawn passenger-carrying vehicles for the use of the superintendent and employees in connection with general park work, and not exceeding $100,000 for the partial construction of a trans-mountain road connecting the east and west sides of the park, $195,000, of which amount $25,000 shall be immediately available.

Grand Canyon National Park, Arizona: For administration, protection, maintenance, improvement, and the acquisition of lands for road and trail rights of way within the park, including not exceeding $2,000 for the purchase, maintenance, operation, and repair of motor-driven passenger-carrying vehicles for the use of the superintendent and employees in connection with general park work, $100,000: *Provided,* That no expenditure shall be made in the maintenance or improvement of any toll road or toll trail.

Hawaii National Park: For administration, protection, maintenance, and improvement, including not exceeding $1,800 for the purchase, maintenance, operation, and repair of a motor-driven passenger-carrying vehicle for use of the superintendent and park employees in connection with general park work, $10,000.

* * * *

Lafayette National Park, Maine: for administration, maintenance, protection, and improvement, including not exceeding $600 for maintenance, operation, and repair of a motor-driven passenger-carrying vehicle for use in administration of the park, $25,000.

Lassen Volcanic National Park, California: For protection and improvement, $3,000.

Mesa Verde National Park, Colorado: For administration, protection, maintenance, and improvement, including not exceeding $800 for maintenance, operation, and repair of horse-drawn and motor-driven passenger-carrying vehicles for use of the superintendent and employees, $16,400.

Mount McKinley National Park, Alaska: For protection and improvement, $8,000.

Mount Rainier National Park, Washington: For administration, protection, maintenance, and improvement, including not exceeding $1,800 for the purchase, maintenance, operation, and repair of motor-driven passenger-carrying vehicles for use of the superintendent and park employees in connection with general park work, not exceeding $2,500 for a ranger station at Paradise Valley; not exceeding $2,500 for a shelter cabin at Camp Muir; $150,000, of which amount $25,000 shall be immediately available.

National Monuments: For the administration, protection, maintenance, preservation, and improvement of the national monuments, to be expended under the direction of the Secretary of the Interior, $12,500.

Platt National Park, Oklahoma: For administration, protection, maintenance, and improvement, $7,500.

Rocky Mountain National Park, Colorado: For administration, protection, maintenance, and improvement, including not exceeding $1,500 for the purchase, maintenance, operation, and repair of motor-driven passenger-carrying vehicles for use of the superintendent and employees in connection with general park work, $65,000.

Sequoia National Park, California: For administration, protection, maintenance, and improvement, including not exceeding $2,000 to be available immediately, for the purchase, maintenance, operation, and repair of a motor-driven passenger-carrying vehicle for the use of the superintendent and employees in connection with general park work, $86,000.

Wind Cave National Park, South Dakota: For administration, protection, maintenance, and improvement, $7,500.

Yellowstone National Park, Wyoming: For administration, protection, maintenance, and improvement, including not to exceed $8,400 for maintenance of the road in the forest reserve leading out of the park from the east boundary, not to exceed $11,000 for purchase and installation of new bridges and culverts for said east forest road, not to exceed $7,500 for maintenance of the road in the forest reserve leading out of the park from the south boundary, not to exceed $16,000 for two combined ranger stations and com-

APPENDICES 93

munity centers for campers at Upper Geyser Basin, Yellowstone Lake, and Grand Canyon, not to exceed $2,500 for fire lookout and rest house on Mount Washburn, not to exceed $7,600 for the purchase, operation, maintenance, and repair of motor-propelled passenger-carrying vehicles, and including feed for buffalo and other animals and salaries of buffalo keepers, $350,000, of which amount $25,000 shall be immediately available, to be expended by and under the direction of the Secretary of the Interior: *Provided,* That not exceeding $2,000 may be expended for the removal of snow from any of the roads for the purpose of opening them in advance of the tourist season.

Yosemite National Park, California: For administration, protection, maintenance, and improvement, including not exceeding $3,000 for purchase, maintenance, operation, and repair of horse-drawn and motor-driven passenger-carrying vehicles for use of the superintendent and employees in connection with general park work, and not exceeding $15,000 for the completion of grading in width not exceeding twenty feet the El Portal-Yosemite road, $300,000.

Zion National Park, Utah: for administration, protection, maintenance, and improvement, $10,000.

Yellowstone

1872—Act of March 1, 1872 (17 Stat. L., 32)—An Act To set aside a certain tract of land lying near the headwaters of the Yellowstone River as a public park.

[SEC. 1]. The tract of land in the Territories of Montana and Wyoming, lying near the head-waters of the Yellowstone River and described as follows, to wit, commencing at the junction of Gardiner's River, with the Yellowstone River, and running east to the meridian passing ten miles to the eastward of the most eastern point of Yellowstone Lake; thence south along said meridian to the parallel of latitude passing ten miles south of the most southern point of Yellowstone Lake; thence west along said parallel to the meridian passing fifteen miles west of the most western point of Madison Lake; thence north along said meridian to the latitude of the junction of the Yellowstone and Gardiner's Rivers; thence east to the place of beginning, is reserved and withdrawn from settlement, occupancy, or sale under the laws of the United States, and dedicated and set apart as a public park or pleasuring-ground for the benefit and enjoyment of the people; and all persons who locate, or settle upon, or occupy any part of the land thus set apart as a public park, except as provided in the following section, shall be considered trespassers and removed therefrom.

SEC. 2. Such public park shall be under the exclusive control of the Secretary of the Interior, whose duty it shall be, as soon as practicable, to make and publish such regulations as he may deem necessary or proper for the care and management of the same.

Such regulations shall provide for the preservation, from injury or spoliation, of all timber, mineral deposits, natural curiosities, or wonders, within the park, and their retention in their natural condition. The Secretary may, in his discretion, grant leases for building purposes, for terms not exceeding ten years, of small parcels of ground, at such places in the park as may require the erection of buildings for the accommodation of visitors; all of the proceeds of such leases, and all other revenues that may be derived from any source connected with the park, to be expended under his direction in the management of the same, and the construction of roads and bridle paths therein. He shall provide against the wanton destruction of the fish and game found within the park, and against their capture or destruction for the purposes of merchandise or profit. He shall also cause all persons trespassing upon the same to be removed therefrom, and generally is authorized to take all such measures as may be necessary or proper to fully carry out the objects and purposes of this section.

1883—Act of March 3, 1883 (22 Stat. L., 626)—An Act Making appropriation for sundry civil expenses of the Government for the fiscal year ending June thirtieth, eighteen hundred and eighty-four, and for other purposes.

Provides for a superintendent and ten assistants to be appointed by the Secretary of the Interior and prescribes their duties; for the construction of roads and bridges under the direction of an engineer officer of the War Department; for the detailing of troops for protection by the Secretary of War at the request of the Secretary of the Interior; and for the leasing, by the Secretary, under definite restrictions, of small tracts for hotel purposes, etc.

1890—Act of July 10, 1890 (26 Stat. L., 222)—An Act To provide for the admission of the State of Wyoming into the union, and for other purposes.

Provides that nothing contained in the act shall be construed as terminating complete federal control and jurisdiction over the park.

1894—Act of May 7, 1894 (28 Stat. L., 73)—An Act To protect the birds and animals in Yellowstone National Park, and to punish crimes in said park and for other purposes.

The act provides for the exclusive jurisdiction of the federal government in the park and that all laws applicable to places under exclusive federal jurisdiction shall be in effect there. It constitutes the park a part of the federal district of Wyoming and provides for the appointment of a Commissioner to reside in the park and try cases therein, and of deputy marshals for the service of process, etc. It also provides for the erection of a building to contain a jail and courtroom. It forbids hunting and fishing, or the killing of any animal except to preserve human life or prevent injury; authorizes the Secretary of the Interior to make rules and regulations for the protection of the game, etc., and prescribes penalties for violation of the act and rules made under it.

1894—Act of August 3, 1894 (28 Stat. L., 222)—An Act Concerning leases in the Yellowstone National Park.

Secretary of the Interior given discretionary authority to make leases in the Park under certain definite restrictions safeguarding the natural wonders from being made the subjects of exclusive privilege. So much of the act of March 3, 1883 as conflicts with the present act is repealed.

1899—Act of March 1, 1899 (30 Stat. L., 918)—An Act To provide compensation for a bridge and for buildings and other improvements constructed by certain persons upon public lands afterwards set apart and reserved as the Yellowstone National Park.

1900—Act of June 6, 1900 (31 Stat. L., 588, 625)—An Act Making appropriations for sundry civil expenses of the Government for the fiscal year ending June thirtieth, nineteen hundred and one, and for other purposes.

That road extensions and improvements shall hereafter be made in said park under and in harmony with a general plan of roads and improvements to be approved by the Chief of Engineers of the Army.

1902—Act of May 27, 1902 (32 Stat. L., 236)—An Act for the allowance of certain claims for stores and supplies reported by the Court of Claims under the provisions of the act approved March 3, 1883, and commonly known as the Bowman Act, and for other purposes.

Provides for the payment to the State of Wyoming of amounts paid out by the State for the policing of the park during 1884, 1885 and 1886.

1903—Act of March 3, 1903 (32 Stat. L., 1130)—An Act Making appropriations for sundry civil expenses of the Government for the fiscal year ending June thirtieth, nineteen hundred and four, and for other purposes.

Conditions prescribed under which private parties or corporations doing business in Yellowstone Park may obtain electric light and power from the government plant.

1906—Act of June 4, 1906 (34 Stat. L., 207)—An Act To amend an act approved August 3, 1894, entitled "An Act concerning leases in the Yellowstone National Park."

Increases the amount of land which may be leased to any one person or company from a possible twenty acres to a possible 200 acres; and permits the mortgaging by any lessee of his rights, properties and franchises, including his contract with the Secretary of the Interior provided the approval of the Secretary be first secured.

1907—Act of March 2, 1907 (34 Stat. L., 1219)—An Act To amend an act entitled "An Act to amend an act approved August 3, 1894, entitled 'An Act concerning leases in the Yellowstone National Park,'" approved June 4, 1906.

Increases leasing period from ten to twenty years.

1911—Act of March 3, 1911 (36 Stat. L., 1087, 1094, 1130)—An Act To codify, revise and amend the laws relating to the judiciary.

Sections 26 and 115 provide for jurisdiction of the federal court for the district of Wyoming over the park; define the district; and provide for terms of court and appointment of deputy marshals.

1916—Act of June 28, 1916 (39 Stat. L., 238)—An Act To

LAWS

amend "An Act to protect the birds and animals in Yellowstone National Park and to punish crimes in said park and for other purposes" approved May 7, eighteen hundred and ninety-four.

Under the old act the penalties for violations of the act or regulations made under it were a fine of not more than $1,000 or imprisonment not exceeding two years, or both, together with all costs, thus classifying all offenses as felonies and necessitating trial of all offenders by indictment in the regular way.

The amendment changed these to $500 or six months, or both, plus costs; thus obviating the necessity for commitments for trial and enabling the park authorities to dispose of cases as they arose by immediate trial before the park commissioner.

1917—Executive Order of April 16, 1917 (No. 2599).

Temporarily withdraws certain lands in Montana north of the park in aid of legislation to secure the lands as a game preserve.

1918—Act of July 1, 1918 (40 Stat. L., 634, 678)—An Act Making appropriations for sundry civil expenses of the Government for the fiscal year ending June thirtieth, nineteen hundred and nineteen, and for other purposes.

Hereafter road extensions and improvements shall be made in said park under and in harmony with the general plan of roads and improvements to be approved by the Secretary of the Interior.

1919—Act of January 25, 1919 (40 Stat. L., 1152)—An Act To authorize the sale of certain lands at or near Yellowstone, Mont., for hotel and other purposes.

Authorizes the sale of eighty-eight acres of land in Madison National Forest to Oregon Short Line Railroad at not less than $25 per acre for use for hotel purposes, provided any hotel erected on tract sold be operated under rules prescribed for operation of hotels in Yellowstone Park.

1919—Executive Order of February 28, 1919 (No. 3053).

Withdraws temporarily the Teton-Jackson's Hole Area south of the Yellowstone in aid of legislation looking to the creation of the proposed greater Yellowstone.

1921—Executive Order of Jan. 28, 1921 (No. 3394).

"Under authority of the act of Congress approved June 25, 1910 (36 Stat. L., 847) as amended by the act of August 24, 1912 (37 Stat. L., 497) the following described lands in the State of Wyoming are hereby temporarily withdrawn, subject to the conditions, provisions and limitations of said acts for the purpose of classifying said lands, and pending enactment of appropriate legislation for their proper disposition."

This order covers the same "Greater Yellowstone" area covered by Executive Order No. 3053, supra; but because it is not made dependent upon any specific legislation its effect is to withdraw the territory indefinitely.

Yosemite

1864—Act of June 30, 1864 (13 Stat. L., 325)—An Act Authorizing a grant to the State of California of the "Yo-Semite Valley" and of the land embracing the "Mariposa Big Tree Grove."

[SEC. 1]. That there . . . is hereby granted to the State of California the "cleft" or "gorge" . . . known as the Yo-Semite Valley . . . with the stipulation, nevertheless, . . . that the premises shall be held for public use, resort and recreation. . . .

SEC. 2. That there shall likewise be, and there is hereby, granted to the said State of California the tracts embracing what is known as the "Mariposa Big Tree Grove" . . . with the like stipulation as expressed in the first section of this act. . . .

1890—Act of October 1, 1890 (36 Stat. L., 650)—An Act To set apart certain tracts of land in the State of California as forest reservations.

[SEC. 1]. That the tracts of land[1] in the State of California . . . are hereby . . . set apart as reserved forest lands. . . . *Provided, however,* That nothing in this act shall be construed as in anywise affecting the grant of lands made to the State of California by virtue of the act entitled "an act authorizing a grant to the state of California of the 'Yo-Semite Valley' and of the land embracing the 'Mariposa Big Tree Grove.' " . . .

SEC. 2. That said reservation shall be under the exclusive control of the Secretary of the Interior, whose duty it shall be . . . to make . . . rules and regulations . . . proper for the care and management of the same. Such regulations shall provide for the preservation of all timber, mineral deposits, natural curiosities or

[1] The lands included in this grant completely surrounded the "cleft" or "gorge" referred to in the Act of June 30, 1864.

wonders within said reservation, and their retention in their natural condition. . . . He shall provide against the wanton destruction of the fish and game . . . and against their capture or destruction for purposes of merchandise or profit. . . .

1892—Act of July 19, 1892 (27 Stat. L., 235)—An Act Granting to the county of Mariposa, in the State of California, the right of way for a free wagon road or turnpike across the Yosemite National Park, in said State.

Land to revert to the United States if road be abandoned or cease to be free of toll.

1900—Act of June 6, 1900 (31 Stat. L., 588, 618)—An Act Making appropriations for sundry civil expenses of the Government for the fiscal year ending June thirtieth, nineteen hundred and one, and for other purposes.

Authorizes Secretary of War upon request of Secretary of the Interior to detail troops to protect the Sequoia, Yosemite, and General Grant Parks.

1901—Act of February 15, 1901 (31 Stat. L., 790)—An Act Relating to rights of way through certain parks, reservations, and other public lands.[1]

Secretary of the Interior authorized to permit and regulate use of rights of way over public lands, forests, and other reservations of the United States, and the Yosemite, Sequoia, and General Grant National Parks for power, telephone, telegraph, irrigation and water supply lines and systems. Grants to be subject to certain provisions and to be revocable at discretion of Secretary.

1904—Act of April 28, 1904 (33 Stat. L., 457, 487)—An Act Making appropriations for sundry civil expenses of the Government for the fiscal year ending June thirtieth, nineteen hundred and five, and for other purposes.

[1] Regulations relating to grants hereunder and under 28 Stat. L., 635, and Sec. 1 of 30 Stat. L., 404 were promulgated by Department of the Interior July 8, 1901.

Directs Secretary of the Interior to ascertain what portions of Yosemite are not necessary for park purposes and to select location for a road.

1905—Act of February 7, 1905 (33 Stat. L., 702)—An Act To exclude from the Yosemite National Park, California, certain lands therein described, and to attach and include the said lands in the Sierra Forest Reserve.

That the tracts of land in the State of California . . . are hereby . . . set apart as reserved forest lands. . . . Provided that the Secretary of the Interior may require the payment of such price as he may deem proper for privileges on the land herein segregated from the Yosemite National Park; . . . and the moneys received from the privileges accorded . . . shall be paid into the Treasury . . . to be expended, under the direction of the Secretary, in the management, improvement and protection of the forest lands herein set aside . . . which shall hereafter be known as the "Yosemite National Park."

1905—Act of March 3, 1905, of the California Legislature.

Receded the Yosemite Valley and Mariposa Big Tree Grove to the United States; recession to take effect from and after acceptance by the United States.

1905—Act of March 3, 1905 (33 Stat. L., 1286)—Joint Resolution Accepting the recession by the State of California of the Yosemite Valley Grant and the Mariposa Big Tree Grove in the Yosemite National Park.

Despite the wording of the above title, the bill as passed merely carried an appropriation for the management, etc., of the Yosemite National Park and said nothing about acceptance of a recession.

1906—Joint Resolution of June 11, 1906 (34 Stat. L., 831)— Joint Resolution accepting the recession by the State of California of the Yosemite Valley Grant and the Mariposa Big Tree Grove, and including the same, together with fractional sections 5 and 6, township 5 south, range 22 east, Mount Diablo meridian, California, within the metes and bounds of the Yosemite

National Park, and changing the boundaries thereof.

[SEC. 1]. That the recession . . . is hereby ratified and accepted, and the tracts . . . are set apart as reserved forest lands . . . and shall hereafter form a part of the Yosemite National Park. . . .

* * * *

SEC. 3. That all revenues . . . shall be paid into the Treasury . . . to be expended . . . in the management, protection, and improvement of the Yosemite National Park.

1910—Act of June 25, 1910 (36 Stat. L., 703, 745)—An Act Making appropriations for sundry civil expenses of the Government for the fiscal year ending June thirtieth, nineteen hundred and eleven, and for other purposes.

$12,000 appropriated to enable Secretary of the Interior to examine data to be submitted by San Francisco in support of a request for a water supply from within Yosemite Park and to collect data independently.

1911—Act of March 4, 1911 (36 Stat. L., 1363, 1420)—An Act Making appropriations for sundry civil expenses of the Government for the fiscal year ending June thirtieth, nineteen hundred and twelve, and for other purposes.

Reappropriates any unexpended balance of appropriation made under Act of June 25, 1910, to enable Secretary to continue the work during fiscal year ending 1912.

1912—Act of April 9, 1912 (37 Stat. L., 80)—An Act To authorize the Secretary of the Interior to secure for the United States title to patented lands in the Yosemite National Park, and for other purposes.

Authorizes the Secretary of the Interior to exchange matured timber in the park for patented lands in park boundaries, prescribes determination of values of lands and timber, and makes regulations for timber cutting and removal. The sale outright of matured timber is also permitted.

1912—Act of August 24, 1912 (37 Stat. L., 417, 460)—An

Act Making appropriations for sundry civil expenses of the Government for the fiscal year ending June thirtieth, nineteen hundred and thirteen, and for other purposes.

Reappropriates any unexpended balance of reappropriation made under act of March 4, 1911 to carry work down to June 30, 1913.

1913—Act of June 23, 1913 (38 Stat. L., 41, 49)—An Act Making appropriation for sundry civil expenses of the Government for the fiscal year ending June thirtieth, nineteen hundred and fourteen.

Authorizes grant of lease by Secretary of Interior for construction, etc., of an hotel and other buildings in accordance with provisions of the act of June 4, 1906, as amended by the act of March 2, 1907. Repeals any part of Sec. 2 of the act of October 1, 1890 concerning the Yosemite in conflict with grant.

1913—Act of December 19, 1913 (38 Stat. L., 242)—An Act Granting to the City and County of San Francisco certain rights of way in, over and through certain public lands, the Yosemite National Park, and Stanislaus National Forest, and certain lands in the Yosemite National Park, the Stanislaus National Forest, and the public lands in the State of California, and for other purposes.

Grants all necessary rights of way in, over and through the Yosemite National Park; together with such lands in the Hetch Hetchy Valley and Lake Eleanor Basin within the Yosemite National Park as Secretary of the Interior may deem to be necessary for reservoirs, such lands as he may deem necessary for power houses, etc., and the right to remove stone, gravel, etc., from the park necessary in the construction of water power and electric plants, etc.

1914—Act of April 16, 1914 (38 Stat. L., 345)—An Act To amend section one of an act of Congress approved April ninth, nineteen hundred and twelve (thirty-seventh statutes, page eighty) entitled "An Act To authorize the Secretary of the Interior to secure for the United States title to patented lands in the Yosemite National Park, and for other purposes."

Empowers the Secretaries of the Interior and of Agriculture to obtain for the United States title to patented lands within the park by exchanging therefor timber or timber and lands within the park and within the adjoining Sierra and Stanislaus National Forests; also to obtain title in similar manner to patented lands not exceeding 640 acres, in said forests, which lands when so acquired shall become part of the Yosemite National Park and be subject to provisions of act of October 1, 1890 (26 Stat. L., 650).

1914—Act of May 13, 1914 (38 Stat. L., 376)—An Act To consolidate certain forest lands in the Sierra National Forest and Yosemite National Park, California.

The Secretary of the Interior is authorized to exchange lands lying in the Sierra National Forest for privately owned lands lying in the Forest and in the Park; lands thus acquired lying in the Forest to go to the Forest and those lying in the Park to go to the Park.

1914—Act of July 23, 1914 (38 Stat. L., 554)—An Act To amend an act approved October 1, 1890, entitled "An Act to set apart certain tracts of land in the State of California as forest reservations."

For hotel purposes, etc., the Secretary of the Interior is authorized to grant leases for not to exceed twenty years on tracts not to exceed twenty acres in extent, not more than ten such tracts to be leased to any one person or corporation. Provision is also made for appraisement at termination of lease and for mortgaging of lessee's rights if desired.

1916—Act of July 1, 1916 (39 Stat. L., 262, 308)—An Act Making appropriation for sundry civil expenses of the Government for the fiscal year ending June thirtieth, nineteen hundred and seventeen, and for other purposes.

Authorization to Secretary of the Interior to accept patented lands and rights of way over same or over other lands in Yosemite Park donated for park purposes.

1918—Executive Order of July 8, 1918 (No. 2906).

Withdraws temporarily the area adjacent to Yosemite Park in aid of pending legislation proposing the creation of a greater park to be called Roosevelt Park.

1920—Act of June 2, 1920 (41 Stat. L., 731)—An Act To accept the cession by the State of California of exclusive jurisdiction of the lands embraced within the Yosemite National Park, Sequoia National Park, and General Grant National Park, respectively, and for other purposes.

Accepts cession of California's Legislature (Act of April 15, 1919). Taxing and process rights reserved to State. Assigns Yosemite to northern California federal judicial district; Sequoia and General Grant to southern. Provides that offenses not prohibited by federal laws be punished by state laws. Prohibits hunting, fishing, spoliation and vandalism and provides penalties. Regulations to be prescribed by Secretary of Interior. Provides for commissioners, defines their powers and outlines procedure. This act is noteworthy in that it amends the National Park Service Act (39 Stat. L., 535) by changing, in Section 3 of said act, the punishment for violations of rules and regulations.

1921—Executive Order of Jan. 28, 1921 (No. 3395).

See Executive Order No. 3394, under the Yellowstone Park, supra. No. 3395 makes what amounts to an indefinite withdrawal of the greater Yosemite or Roosevelt area (See Executive Order No. 2906) in the same terms employed in No. 3394.

Sequoia

1890—Act of September 25, 1890 (26 Stat. L., 478)—An Act To set apart a certain tract of land in the State of California as a public park.

[SEC. 1]. That the tract[1] of land in the State of California . . . is hereby . . . set apart as a public park, or pleasure ground, for the benefit and enjoyment of the people. . . .
SEC. 2. That said public park shall be under the exclusive control of the Secretary of the Interior, whose duty it shall be . . . to make rules and regulations . . . for the care and management of the same. Such regulations shall provide for the preservation

[1] This act covers part of Sequoia: the remainder is reserved by Section 3 of the Act of October 1, 1890 (26 Stat. L., 650).

LAWS

from injury of all timber, mineral deposits, natural curiosities or wonders within said park, and their retention in their natural condition. . . . He shall provide against the wanton destruction of fish and game and against their capture or destruction for purposes of merchandise or profit. . . .

1890—Act of October 1, 1890 (26 Stat. L., 650)—An Act To set apart certain tracts of land in the State of California as forest reservations.

See this same act under Yosemite, to which park the first two sections thereof relate. The third section sets aside as part of Sequoia Park the following: Twps. 15 and 16 S., Rs 29 and 30 E., Mount Diablo base and meridian, and all of Twp. 17 S., R. 30 E., with the exception of Sects. 31 to 34 inclusive, the lands forming the remainder of the park being reserved by the act of September 25, 1890 (26 Stat. L., 478) supra, which see.

1900—Act of June 6, 1900 (31 Stat. L., 618)—An Act Making appropriation for sundry civil expenses of the Government for the fiscal year ending June thirtieth, nineteen hundred and one, and for other purposes.

See same act under Yosemite.

1901—Act of February 15, 1901 (31 Stat. L., 790)—An Act Relating to rights of way through certain parks, reservations and other public lands.

See same act under Yosemite.

1914—Act of August 1, 1914 (38 Stat. L., 609, 649)—An Act Making appropriations for sundry civil expenses the Government for the fiscal year ending June thirtieth, nineteen hundred and fifteen, and for other purposes.

Authorizes the Secretary of the Interior to accept rights of way over patented lands within Sequoia Park.

1916—Act of July 1, 1916 (39 Stat. L., 262, 308)—An Act Making appropriations for sundry civil expenses of the Government for the fiscal year ending June thirtieth, nineteen hundred and seventeen, and for other purposes.

Authorization to accept gifts of patented lands or rights of way over same or over other lands in Sequoia Park given to Secretary of the Interior.

1920—Act of June 2, 1920 (41 Stat. L., 731)—An Act To accept the cession by the State of California of exclusive jurisdiction of the lands embraced within the Yosemite National Park, Sequoia National Park and General Grant National Park, respectively, and for other purposes.

See same act under Yosemite.

General Grant

1890—Act of October 1, 1890 (26 Stat. L., 650)—An Act To set apart certain tracts of land in the State of California as forest reservations.

See this same act under Yosemite, to which park the first two sections of the act relate. The third section sets aside a portion of Sequoia Park and the following tracts for General Grant Park: Sects. 5 and 6, Twp. 14 S., R. 28 E., and Sects. 31 and 32, Twp. 13 S., R. 28 E., Mount Diablo base and meridian. The reservation is made under the same limitations, restrictions and provisions that apply to Sequoia and Yosemite.

1900—Act of June 6, 1900 (31 Stat. L., 588, 618)—An Act Making appropriation for sundry civil expenses of the Government for the fiscal year ending June thirtieth, nineteen hundred and one, and for other purposes.

See same act under Yosemite.

1901—Act of February 15, 1901 (31 Stat. L., 790)—An Act Relating to rights of way through certain parks, reservations and other public lands.

See same act under Yosemite.

LAWS 107

1920—Act of June 2, 1920 (41 Stat. L., 731)—An Act To accept the cession by the State of California of exclusive jurisdiction of the lands embraced within the Yosemite National Park, Sequoia National Park, and General Grant National Park, respectively, and for other purposes.
See same act under Yosemite.

Mount Rainier

1899—Act of March 2, 1899 (30 Stat. L., 993)—An Act To set aside a portion of certain lands in the State of Washington now known as the "Pacific Forest Reserve," as a public park, to be known as the "Mount Rainier National Park."

[SEC. 1]. That all those certain tracts . . . in the State of Washington . . . are hereby . . . set aside as a public park to be known and designated as the "Mount Rainier National Park."

SEC. 2. That said public park shall be under the exclusive control of the Secretary of the Interior, whose duty it shall be to make and publish, as soon as practicable, such rules and regulations as he may deem necessary or proper for the care and management of the same. Such regulations shall provide for the preservation from injury or spoliation of all timber, mineral deposits, natural curiosities, or wonders within said park and their retention in their natural condition. . . . He shall provide against the wanton destruction of the fish and game found within said park, and against their capture or destruction for purposes of merchandise or profit.
* * * *

SEC. 5. That the mineral land laws of the United States are hereby extended to the lands lying within the said reserve and said park.[1]

The act also provides for the granting of leases, etc., by the Secretary of the Interior, and stipulates that all revenue derived from the park shall be expended on its improvement. It also authorizes the Secretary to grant rights of way at his discretion.

Settlers in the park and railroads owning lands therein are given lieu land selection privileges.

1908—Act of May 27, 1908 (35 Stat. L., 365)—An Act Making appropriations for sundry civil expenses of the Government for the fiscal year ending June

[1] Further location prohibited by Act of May 27, 1908 (35 Stat. L., 365).

thirtieth, nineteen hundred and nine, and for other purposes.

Prohibits location of further mining claims in Mt. Rainier Park, but provides that claims theretofore acquired in good faith under mineral laws shall not be affected.

1916—Act of June 30, 1916 (39 Stat. L., 243)—An Act To accept the cession by the State of Washington of exclusive jurisdiction over the lands embraced within the Mount Rainier National Park, and for other purposes.

Accepts, cession in usual terms (Act of Washington Legislature March 16, 1901) reserving process and taxing rights to State. Placed in western Washington federal judicial district. Washington laws to control where there is no federal prohibition of an offense. Prohibition of hunting, fishing, spoliation and vandalism, and penalties prescribed. Secretary of the Interior to make Regulations. Commissioner provided for and powers defined. Procedure outlined.

1917—Act of June 12, 1917 (40 Stat. L., 105, 152)—An Act Making appropriations for sundry civil expenses of the Government for the fiscal year ending June thirtieth, nineteen hundred and eighteen, and for other purposes.

Authorizes acceptance by Secretary of the Interior of patented lands or rights of way over same in Mount Rainier Park donated for park purposes. Similar authorization in same act covering Rocky Mountain, Mesa Verde, and Crater Lake Parks.

Crater Lake

1902—Act of May 22, 1902 (32 Stat. L., 202)—An Act Reserving from the public lands in the State of Oregon, as a public park for the benefit of the people of the United States, and for the protection and preservation of the game, fish, timber, and all other natural objects therein, a tract of land herein described, and so forth.

[SEC. 1]. That the tract of land . . . in the State of Oregon, and including Crater Lake is hereby . . . set apart forever as a public park or pleasure ground for the benefit of the people of the United States, to be known as "Crater Lake National Park."

SEC. 2. That the reservation established by this act shall be under the control and custody of the Secretary of the Interior, whose duty it shall be to establish rules and regulations and cause adequate measures to be taken for the preservation of the natural objects within said park, and also for the protection of the timber from wanton depredation, the preservation of all kinds of game and fish, the punishment of trespassers, the removal of unlawful occupants and intruders, and the prevention and extinguishment of forest fires.

The act further forbids all residence and settlement and the engaging in business or speculative enterprises; with the proviso that the park shall be open to "scientists, excursionists and pleasure seekers," and to the locating and working of mining claims; and with the further proviso that restaurant and hotel keepers may operate in the park at the discretion of the Secretary of the Interior. The act also prescribes penalties for its violation or the violation of rules made under it.

1916—Act of August 21, 1916 (39 Stat. L., 521)—An Act To accept the cession by the State of Oregon of exclusive jurisdiction over the lands embraced within the Crater Lake National Park, and for other purposes.

Accepts cession of sole jurisdiction to the United States (reserving process and taxing rights to State). Places park in the Oregon federal judicial district. Prohibits hunting, fishing, spoliation and vandalism and provides penalties for violations of regulations. Provides for appointment of a United States Commissioner, defines his powers, and outlines procedure.

1917—Act of June 12, 1917 (40 Stat. L., 105, 152)—An Act Making appropriations for sundry civil expenses of the Government for the fiscal year ending June thirtieth, nineteen hundred and eighteen, and for other purposes.

See same act under Mount Rainier.

Wind Cave

1903—Act of January 9, 1903 (32 Stat. L., 765)—An Act To set apart certain lands in the State of South

Dakota as a public park to be known as the "Wind Cave National Park."

* * * *

SEC. 2. That said park shall be known as the "Wind Cave National Park" and shall be under the exclusive control of the Secretary of the Interior, whose duty it shall be to prescribe such rules and regulations and establish such service as he may deem necessary for the care and management of the same.

The act also authorizes the granting of leases by the Secretary, prescribes punishment for offenses, provides for the protection of preëxisting land rights and stipulates that all funds derived from rentals, etc., shall be used in the care of the park.

1912—Act of August 10, 1912 (37 Stat. L., 269, 293)—An Act Making appropriations for the Department of Agriculture for the fiscal year ending June thirtieth, nineteen hundred and thirteen, and for other purposes.

* * * *

For the establishment of a national game preserve . . . within the . . . Wind Cave National Park . . . etc.; $26,000.

1920—Executive Order of July 14, 1920 (No. 3308).

Makes temporary withdrawal under authority of the Act of June 25, 1910, as amended by the Act of August 24, 1912, in order to protect water supply of Wind Cave Park and the bison range therein.

Platt

1902—Act of July 1, 1902 (32 Stat. L., 641, 655)—An Act To ratify and confirm an agreement with the Choctaw and Chickasaw tribes of Indians, and for other purposes.

By a clause in the agreement the two tribes ceded to the United States the tract near the village of Sulphur, in the Chickasaw Nation containing the mineral springs, the whole aggregating in area about 640 acres. The act charges the Secretary of the Interior with the making of rules for the regulation and control of the use of the waters.

1904—Act of April 21, 1904 (33 Stat. L., 189, 220)—An Act Making appropriations for the current and contingent expenses of the Indian Department and for fulfilling treaty stipulations with various Indian tribes for the fiscal year ending June thirtieth, nineteen hundred and five, and for other purposes.

Authorization to Secretary of the Interior to add to the original Platt reservation Act of July 1, 1902, some two hundred acres lying adjacent thereto; and to place a representative on the land to enforce rules and regulations for the control and use thereof and of the waters of the springs and creeks.

1906—Act of June 16, 1906 (34 Stat. L., 267)—An Act To enable the people of Oklahoma and of the Indian Territory to form a Constitution and State government, etc.

Retains (Sects. 3, 7 and 13), national jurisdiction over the Sulphur Springs Reservation reserving to the state thereafter to be created the right of process.

1906—Joint Resolution of June 29, 1906 (34 Stat. L., 837)— Joint Resolution directing that the Sulphur Springs Reservation be named and hereafter called the "Platt National Park."

Secretary of the Interior authorized to make the change in name in honor of Orville Hitchcock Platt, for many years a member of the Senate Committee on Indian Affairs.

Sullys Hill

1904—Act of April 27, 1904 (33 Stat. L., 323)—An Act To modify and amend an agreement with the Indians of the Devil's Lake Reservation, in North Dakota, to accept and ratify the same as amended, and making appropriation and provision to carry the same into effect.

The President is also authorized to reserve a tract embracing Sullys Hill, in the northeastern portion of the abandoned military reservation, about nine hundred and sixty acres, as a public park.

112 THE NATIONAL PARK SERVICE

1904—Presidential Proclamation of June 2, 1904. No. 32 (33 Stat. L., 2370).

The proclamation, in pursuance of the authority granted in the Act of April 27, 1904, throws open the Devils Lake Indian Reservation to settlement, reserving certain lands for various purposes, among them the following:
"Lots 4, 5, 6 and 7 of Sect. 10, the NW¼, the W½ of the SW¼, and lots 5 and 6 of Sect. 15, lots 1 and 2 of Sect. 9, the E½ of the NE¼, the SE¼ of the SE¼ and lots 3, 4 and 5 of Sect. 16, T 152 N., R 65 W., of the fifth principal meridian, which are hereby reserved for public use as a park to be known as Sullys Hill Park."

1914—Act of June 30, 1914 (38 Stat. L., 415, 434)—An Act Making appropriations for the Department of Agriculture for the fiscal year ending June thirtieth, nineteen hundred and fifteen.

Authorizes establishment of a game preserve in Sullys Hill Park.

Mesa Verde

1906—Act of June 29, 1906 (34 Stat. L., 616)—An Act Creating the Mesa Verde National Park.

[Sec. 1]. That there is hereby . . . set aside as a public reservation all those certain tracts . . . in the State of Colorado. . . .

Sec. 2. That said public park shall be known as the Mesa Verde National Park, and shall be under the exclusive control of the Secretary of the Interior, whose duty it shall be to prescribe such rules and regulations and establish such service as he may deem necessary for the care and management of the same. Such regulations shall provide specifically for the preservation from injury or spoilation of the ruins and other works and relics of prehistoric or primitive man within said park.

The act further provides that the Secretary may permit excavating, etc., by properly qualified persons for the benefit of some reputable museum or educational institution with a view to promoting archæological science.

The act also provides for the punishment of persons destroying or molesting the ruins; and stipulates that all ruins situated within five miles of the park boundaries, unless on land regularly alienated, shall be under the jurisdiction of the superintendent. This last provision was repealed by the act of June 30, 1913 (38 Stat. L., 84).

1910—Act of June 25, 1910 (36 Stat. L., 774, 796)—An Act Making appropriations to supply deficiencies in

LAWS 113

appropriations for the fiscal year 1910, and for other purposes.

Permits the Secretary of the Interior to grant leases, etc., in Mesa Verde Park, provided land including ruins be not leased and public not denied free access thereto.

1913—Act of June 30, 1913 (38 Stat. L., 77, 82)—An Act Making appropriations for the current and contingent expenses of the Bureau of Indian Affairs for fulfilling treaty stipulations with various Indian tribes and for other purposes, for the fiscal year ending June thirtieth, nineteen hundred and fourteen.

An agreement of May 10, 1911 made at Navajo Springs agency, Colorado, with a portion of the Ute Indian tribe amended and confirmed. It provided for an exchange of Indian lands for certain lands within the park—the Indian lands to become park lands and the park lands to become part of the Indians' reservation. So much of the Act of June 29, 1906 (34 Stat. L., 617) as extends jurisdiction of Secretary of Interior five miles from park borders repealed.

1917—Act of June 12, 1917 (40 Stat. L., 105, 152)—An Act Making appropriations for sundry civil expenses of the Government for the fiscal year ending June thirtieth, nineteen hundred and eighteen, and for other purposes.

See same act under Mount Rainier.

Glacier

1910—Act of May 11, 1910 (36 Stat. L., 354)—An Act To establish "The Glacier National Park" in the Rocky Mountains South of the International Boundary Line, in the State of Montana, and for other purposes.

[SEC. 1]. That the tract of land in the State of Montana . . . is hereby . . . set apart as a public park or pleasure ground for . . . the people of the United States under the name of "The Glacier National Park."

SEC. 2. That said park shall be under the executive control of the Secretary of the Interior, whose duty it shall be, as soon as practicable, to make and publish such rules and regulations not inconsistent with the laws of the United States as he may deem necessary or proper for the care, protection, management, and improvement of the same, which regulations shall provide for the preservation of the park in a state of nature so far as is consistent with the purposes of this act, and for the care and protection of the fish and game within the boundaries thereof.

Further, the act safeguards preëxisting land rights; permits the acquisition of rights of way and the utilization of park areas by the United States Reclamation Service; authorizes the Secretary to make leases and sell matured timber; and denies to railroads or other corporations owning land within the park the right to use such ownership as a basis for indemnity selection in any State or Territory.

1911—Act of March 4, 1911 (36 Stat. L., 1363, 1421)—An Act Making appropriations for sundry civil expenses of the Government for the fiscal year ending June thirtieth, nineteen hundred and twelve, and for other purposes.

Permits expenditure of park revenues for park administration and improvement.

1912—Act of February 10, 1912 (37 Stat. L., 64)—An Act To authorize the sale of land within or near the town of Midvale, Montana, for hotel purposes.

Authorizes sale of not to exceed 160 acres at not less than $25 per acre, any hotel erected thereon to be operated under rules prescribed by Secretary of Interior for operation of hotels in Glacier Park. Withdrawal of not to exceed five acres in town of Midvale for use in administrative purposes of Glacier National Park also authorized.

1914—Act of August 1, 1914 (38 Stat. L., 609, 649)—An Act Making appropriations for sundry civil expenses of the Government for the fiscal year ending June thirtieth, nineteen hundred and fifteen, and for other purposes.

Authorization for acceptance of rights of way over patented lands in Glacier Park. This authorization is repeated in 38 Stat. L., 863, the Sundry Civil Act of March 3, 1915 for fiscal year ending June 30, 1916.

LAWS

1914—Act of August 22, 1914 (38 Stat. L., 699)—An Act To accept the cession by the State of Montana of exclusive jurisdiction over the lands embraced within the Glacier National Park, and for other purposes.

The act accepts jurisdiction, reserving to the State rights of process and taxation, and placing the park in the federal district for Montana. It makes prohibitions regarding hunting, fishing, spoliation, etc., and prescribes penalties. Provision is made for the appointment of a Commissioner, and his powers, etc., are outlined.

1915—Act of February 27, 1915 (38 Stat. L., 814)—An Act To authorize the Great Northern Railway Company to revise the location of its right of way, and for other purposes.

Grant made subject to limitations contained in act of March 3, 1875 (18 Stat. L., 482) as amended by act of March 3, 1899 (30 Stat. L., 1233).

1916—Act of July 1, 1916 (39 Stat. L., 262, 308)—An Act Making appropriations for sundry civil expenses of the Government for the fiscal year ending June thirtieth, nineteen hundred and seventeen, and for other purposes.

Authorization to Secretary of Interior to accept patented lands or rights over same located in Glacier Park that may be donated for park purposes.

1916—Act of July 3, 1916 (39 Stat. L., 342)—An Act For the relief of certain homestead entrymen for land within the limits of the Glacier National Park.

Entries of certain homesteaders excepted from force of act creating park, with proviso for reversion to park in case of non-perfection.

1917—Act of March 2, 1917 (39 Stat. L., 916)—An Act To authorize the sale of certain lands at or near Belton, Montana, for hotel purposes.

Sale of portion of a half of a quarter section at not less than $25 per acre to Glacier Park Hotel Co. authorized, provided any hotel erected on land sold be operated under rules prescribed for hotels within Glacier Park.

1917—Act of March 3, 1917 (39 Stat. L., 1122)—An Act To authorize an exchange of lands with owners of private holdings within the Glacier National Park.

Authorizes the Secretary of the Interior to exchange for privately held lands within the park boundaries matured timber of an equal value on park lands, that can be removed without injury to the park; or, with the assent of the Secretary of Agriculture, timber from the adjoining national forest.

1917—Act of June 12, 1917 (40 Stat. L., 105, 151)—An Act Making appropriations for sundry civil expenses of the Government for the fiscal year ending June thirtieth, nineteen hundred and eighteen, and for other purposes.

Authorizes acceptance by the Secretary of the Interior of donations for park purposes of "buildings, money and other property which may be useful in the betterment of the administration and affairs of the Glacier National Park under his supervision."

Rocky Mountain

1915—Act of January 26, 1915 (38 Stat. L., 798)—An Act To establish the Rocky Mountain National Park in the State of Colorado, and for other purposes.

[SEC. 1]. That the tract of land in the State of Colorado . . . is hereby reserved and withdrawn from settlement, occupancy, or disposal under the laws of the United States, and said tract is dedicated and set apart as a public park for the benefit and enjoyment of the people of the United States, under the name of the Rocky Mountain National Park: *Provided,* That the United States Reclamation Service may enter upon and utilize for flowage or other purposes any area within said park which may be necessary for the development and maintenance of a Government reclamation project.
* * * *

SEC. 4. That the said park shall be under the executive control of the Secretary of the Interior, and it shall be the duty of the said executive authority, as soon as practicable, to make and publish such reasonable rules and regulations, not inconsistent with the laws of

LAWS

the United States, as the said authority may deem necessary or proper for the care, protection, management, and improvement of the same, the said regulations being primarily aimed at the freest use of the said park for recreation purposes by the public and the preservation of the natural conditions and scenic beauties thereof. The said authority may, in his discretion, execute leases to parcels of ground not exceeding twenty acres in extent in any one place to any person or company for not to exceed twenty years whenever such ground is necessary for the erection of establishments for the accommodation of visitors, may grant such other necessary privileges and concessions as he deems wise for the accommodation of visitors, and may likewise arrange for the removal of such mature or dead or down timber as he may deem necessary and advisable for the protection and improvement of the park. The regulations governing the park shall include provisions for the use of automobiles therein: *Provided,* That no appropriation for the maintenance, supervision or improvement of said park in excess of $10,000 annually shall be made unless the same shall have first been expressly authorized by law.[1]

The act also provided for the non-impairment of theretofore existing land entries; and the granting of rights of way for transportation lines across the park by the Secretary of the Interior at his discretion. It also provides that privately held lands within the park shall not be affected by the law, and that when not inconsistent with primary purposes of the park the law regarding irrigational rights of way the act of Feb. 15, 1901 (31 Stat. L., 790) shall be applicable to the park.

1917—Act of February 14, 1917 (39 Stat. L., 916)—An Act To add certain lands to Rocky Mountain National Park, Colorado.

1917—Act of June 12, 1917 (40 Stat. L., 105, 152)—An Act Making appropriations for sundry civil expenses of the Government for the fiscal year ending June thirtieth, nineteen hundred and eighteen, and for other purposes.

See same act under Mount Rainier.

1919—Act of March 1, 1919 (40 Stat. L., 1270)—An Act To repeal the last proviso of Section 4 of an Act to establish the Rocky Mountain National Park, in the State of Colorado, and for other purposes, approved January twenty-sixth, nineteen hundred and fifteen.

[1] Proviso repealed by Act of March 1, 1919 (40 Stat. L., 1271).

Removes $10,000 limitation on appropriations.

Hawaii

1916—Act of August 1, 1916 (39 Stat. L., 432)—An Act To establish a national park in the Territory of Hawaii.

Sets aside tracts on islands of Hawaii and Maui as a "public park or pleasure ground," etc., "to be known as Hawaii National Park." Provides for administration under the Secretary of the Interior, granting of leases, disposition of revenues, etc. Limits appropriations to $10,000 unless express authorization be had, also provides that no appropriation shall be made until such perpetual easements and rights of way over privately owned lands in the park shall be transferred to the United States as shall make the park reasonably accessible.

1920—Act of February 20, 1920 (41 Stat. L., 452)—An Act To authorize the governor of the Territory of Hawaii to acquire privately owned lands and rights of way within the boundaries of the Hawaii National Park.

Acquisition to be at the expense of Territory of Hawaii, by exchange or otherwise; and provisions of Section 73 of the act of April 30, 1900, as amended by the act of May 27, 1910, regarding exchange of public lands, not to apply.

Lassen Volcanic

1916—Act of August 9, 1916 (39 Stat. L., 442)—An Act To establish the Lassen Volcanic National Park in the Sierra Nevada Mountains in the State of California, and for other purposes.

[SEC. 1]. . . , That all those certain tracts . . . of land . . . are set aside as a public park or pleasuring-ground for the people of the United States. . . .
SEC. 2. That said park shall be under the exclusive control of the Secretary of the Interior, whose duty it shall be, as soon as practicable, to make and publish such rules and regulations not inconsistent with the laws of the United States as he may deem necessary or proper for the care, protection, management, and improvement of the same. Such regulations being primarily aimed at the freest

use of said park for recreation purposes by the public and for the preservation from injury or spoliation of all timber, mineral deposits, and natural curiosities or wonders within said park and their retention in their natural condition as far as practicable and for the preservation of the park in a state of nature so far as is consistent with the purposes of this Act. He shall provide against the wanton destruction of the fish and game found within said park and against their capture or destruction for purposes of merchandise or profit, and generally shall be authorized to take all such measures as shall be necessary to fully carry out the objects and purposes of this Act. . . .

The act also provides against appropriations of more than $5,000 annually unless expressly authorized. It also authorizes the Secretary of the Interior to grant leases for the accommodation of visitors and to exact charges for same and to sell dead, matured, and down timber. Trespassing is forbidden. Provisos are inserted safeguarding privately owned lands and valid preëxisting entries. Reclamation Service use is permitted and provision is made for the acquisition of rights of way by railways, for automobile roads, etc. Lands in the park not to be used as a basis for claims of indemnity selection by corporations.

Mount McKinley

1917—Act of February 26, 1917 (39 Stat. L., 938)—An Act To establish the Mount McKinley National Park in the Territory of Alaska.

SEC. 1. . . . and said tract is dedicated and set apart as a public park for the benefit and enjoyment of the people, under the name of the Mount McKinley National Park.

* * * *

SEC. 5. That the said park shall be under the executive control of the Secretary of the Interior, and it shall be the duty of the said executive authority, as soon as practicable, to make and publish such rules and regulations not inconsistent with the laws of the United States as the said authority may deem necessary or proper for the care, protection, management, and improvement of the same, the said regulations being primarily aimed at the freest use of the said park for recreation purposes by the public and for the preservation of animals, birds, and fish and for the preservation of the natural curiosities and scenic beauties thereof.

* * * *

SEC. 8. That any person found guilty of violating any of the provisions of this Act shall be deemed guilty of a misdemeanor, and shall be subjected to a fine of not more than $500 or imprisonment not exceeding six months, or both, and be adjudged to pay all costs of the proceedings.

The act also provides against the impairment of preëxisting land entries, states that the mineral land laws shall remain in force as regards the park; permits locations of rights of way under the act of February 15, 1901 (31 Stat. L., 790); establishes park as a game refuge, with the proviso that killing for actual food necessities is permitted; provides for the execution of leases of not to exceed twenty acres for not to exceed twenty years; and limits maintenance appropriations to $10,000 annually unless previously authorized by law.

Grand Canyon

1919—Act of February 26, 1919 (40 Stat. L., 1175)—An Act To establish the Grand Canyon National Park in the State of Arizona.

* * * *

SEC. 2. That the administration, protection, and promotion of said Grand Canyon National Park shall be exercised, under the direction of the Secretary of the Interior, by the National Park Service, subject to the provisions of the act of August twenty-fifth, nineteen hundred and sixteen, entitled "An Act to establish a National Park Service, and for other purposes": *Provided,* That all concessions for hotels, camps, transportation, and other privileges of every kind and nature for the accommodation or entertainment of visitors shall be let at public bidding to the best and most responsible bidder.[1]

* * * *

SEC. 4. That nothing herein contained shall affect any valid existing claim, location, or entry under the land laws of the United States, whether for homestead, mineral, right of way, or any other purposes whatsoever, or shall affect the rights of any such claimant, locator, or entryman to the full use and enjoyment of his land and nothing herein contained shall affect, diminish, or impair the right and authority of the county of Coconino, in the State of Arizona, to levy and collect tolls for the passage of live stock over and upon the Bright Angel Toll Road and Trail, and the Secretary of the Interior is hereby authorized to negotiate with the said County of Coconino for the purchase of said Bright Angel Toll Road and Trail and all rights therein, and report to Congress at as early a date as possible the terms upon which the property can be procured.

* * * *

SEC. 6. That whenever consistent with the primary purposes of said park, the Secretary of the Interior is authorized, under general regulations to be prescribed by him, to permit the prospecting, development, and utilization of the mineral resources of said park upon such terms and for specified periods, or otherwise, as he may deem to be for the best interests of the United States.

SEC. 7. That, whenever consistent with the primary purposes of said park, the Secretary of the Interior is authorized to permit the

---

[1] See Sect. 3 of Act of August 25, 1916 (39 Stat. L., 535) the National Park Service Act.

utilization of areas therein which may be necessary for the development and maintenance of a Government reclamation project.

The act also provides for the granting of rights of way for railroads across the park at the discretion of the Secretary of the Interior; the continuation of the existing rights of the Havasupai Indians; the revoking of the executive order creating the Grand Canyon National Monument; and the exclusion of all parts of the park from the Grand Canyon Game Preserve.

Lafayette

1919—Act of February 26, 1919 (40 Stat. L., 1178)—An Act To establish the Lafayette National Park in the State of Maine.

Declares Sieur de Monts National Monument to be a national park under name of Lafayette National Park and provides for its administration by the National Park Service. Also authorizes the Secretary of the Interior to accept donations for the extension or improvement of the park.

Zion

1919—Act of November 19, 1919 (41 Stat. L., 356)—An Act To establish the Zion National Park in the State of Utah.

[SEC. 1]. That the Zion National Monument, in the county of Washington, State of Utah, established and designated as a national monument under the act of June 8, 1906, entitled "An Act for the preservation of American antiquities," by presidential proclamations of July 31, 1909, and March 18, 1918, is hereby declared to be a national park and dedicated as such for the benefit and enjoyment of the people under the name of the Zion National Park, under which name the aforesaid national park shall be maintained by allotment of funds heretofore or hereafter appropriated for the national monuments, until such time as an independent appropriation is made therefor by Congress.

SEC. 2. That the administration, protection, and promotion of said Zion National Park shall be exercised under the direction of the Secretary of the Interior by the National Park Service, subject to the provision of the Act of August 25, 1916, entitled "An Act to establish a National Park Service and for other purposes," and acts additional thereto or amendatory thereof.

Hot Springs

1832—Act of April 20, 1832 (4 Stat. L., 505)—An Act

authorizing the governor of the Territory of Arkansas to lease the salt springs, in said territory, and for other purposes.

SEC. 3. That the hot springs, in said territory, together with four sections of land including said springs, as near the center thereof as may be, shall be reserved for the future disposal of the United States, and shall not be entered, located, or appropriated, for any purpose whatever.

1870—Act of June 11, 1870 (16 Stat. L., 149)—An Act In relation to the Hot Springs Reservation in Arkansas.

Provides for the prosecution in the Court of Claims of suits against the United States by persons claiming title to land in the Hot Springs Reservation.

1877—Act of March 3, 1877 (19 Stat. L., 377)—An Act In relation to the Hot Springs Reservation in the State of Arkansas.

Provides for the appointment of three Commissioners to dispose of —by sale after appraisement—all of Hot Springs Reservation except an area including all the hot springs; said area to be reserved from sale and to remain in charge of a superintendent to be appointed by the Secretary of the Interior.

The act also grants a right of way to the Hot Springs Railroad Company, and sets aside not to exceed five acres—from the land to be sold—for the use of Garland County, Arkansas, as a site for a public building.

1878—Act of December 16, 1878 (20 Stat. L., 258)—An Act To correct an error of enrollment in bill making appropriations for sundry civil expenses of the Government for the fiscal year ending June thirtieth 1879, and for other purposes.

Revives and continues in force act of March 3, 1877, provides for the appointment of three commissioners, and prescribes rules for the leasing of hot water privileges.

1880—Act of June 16, 1880 (21 Stat. L., 288)—An Act

LAWS 123

For the establishment of titles in Hot Springs, and for other purposes.

* * * *

SEC. 3. That those divisions of the Hot Springs Reservation, known as the mountainous districts, not divided by streets on the maps made by the commissioners, but known and defined on the map and in the report of the Commissioners as North Mountain, West Mountain, and Sugar Loaf Mountain, be, and the same are hereby forever reserved from sale, and dedicated to public use as parks, to be known, with Hot Springs Mountain, as the permanent reservation.

1881—Act of March 3, 1881 (26 Stat. L., 842)—An Act To regulate the granting of leases at Hot Springs, Arkansas, and for other purposes.

Grants full powers to the Secretary of the Interior in connection with the leasing of hot water rights, sale of lots, etc.

1882—Act of June 30, 1882 (22 Stat. L., 121)—An Act Making appropriations for the support of the Army for the fiscal year ending June thirtieth, eighteen hundred and eighty-three, and for other purposes.

Provides for the erection of an Army and Navy Hospital on the reservation at Hot Springs.

1882—Act of July 8, 1882 (22 Stat. L., 155)—An Act To authorize the sale of certain lots in the city of Hot Springs, Arkansas, to the Women's Christian National Library Association.

1887—Joint Resolution of March 3, 1887 (24 Stat. L., 647)—Joint Resolution To authorize the use of hot water off the Government Reservation at Hot Springs, Arkansas.

Authorizes the Secretary of the Interior to continue to supply hot water to bath houses located off the permanent reservation.

1888—Joint Resolution of March 26, 1888 (25 Stat. L., 619)—Joint Resolution To enable the Secretary of

THE NATIONAL PARK SERVICE

the Interior to utilize the hot water now running to waste on the permanent reservation at Hot Springs, Arkansas, and for other purposes.

1888—Act of October 19, 1888 (25 Stat. L., 609)—An Act Granting the right of way for the construction of a railroad through the Hot Springs Reservation, State of Arkansas.

Leave granted the Mountain View Railway Co., of Hot Springs, to build line of railway across reservation. Conditions prescribed. Reservation by government of right to amend, add to, alter or repeal.

1892—Act of June 22, 1892 (27 Stat. L., 58)—An Act To include lot numbered 53 in block 89, at Hot Springs, Arkansas, in the public reservation at that place.

1892—Act of July 14, 1892 (27 Stat. L., 174)—An Act To grant lot numbered one in block numbered 72 of the Hot Springs Reservation to the school district of the city of Hot Springs for school purposes.

1892—Act of August 5, 1892 (27 Stat. L., 373)—An Act Making appropriations for sundry civil expenses of the Government for the fiscal year ending June thirtieth, eighteen hundred and ninety-three, and for other purposes.

Provision made for improvement of reservation and to make same available as a reservoir to retain flood waters of Hot Springs Creek.

1893—Act of December 21, 1893 (28 Stat. L., 21)—An Act Granting the right of way for the construction of a railroad and other improvements over and on the West Mountain of the Hot Springs Reservation, Hot Springs, Arkansas.

Grants right of way to George W. Baxter et al as well as hotel privilege and use of five acres on reservation for a park. Rental

LAWS 125

of two per cent on gross earnings per annum to be paid to Secretary of Interior, who has supervision over rates to be charged. Right to alter, amend, etc., reserved by Congress.

1894—Act of June 21, 1894 (28 Stat. L., 95)--An Act Granting the use of certain lands in the Hot Springs Reservation, in the State of Arkansas, to the Barry Hospital.

Use only granted. Fee retained by the Government and right to resume possession.

1894—Act of August 7, 1894 (28 Stat. L., 263)—An Act Authorizing the Secretary of the Interior to grant leases for sites on the Hot Springs Reservation, Arkansas, for cold water reservoirs.

Lease to Hot Springs Water Co., or any other person or corporation authorized for not to exceed twenty years. Renewal for like period allowed.

1894—Act of August 9, 1894 (28 Stat. L., 274)—An Act To authorize sale of lot eight, block ninety-three, city of Hot Springs, by school directors thereof, and use of proceeds for school purposes.

1894—Act of August 11, 1894 (28 Stat. L., 1004)—An Act For the relief of Henry James residing in the original Hot Springs Reservation, in the State of Arkansas.

Right granted to purchase improved lot.

1896—Act of February 15, 1896 (29 Stat. L., 7)—An Act To extend the time for the completion of the incline railway on West Mountain, Hot Springs Reservation.

Three years extension of time granted. Act of December 21, 1893 continued in full force and effect.

1898—Act of March 19, 1898 (30 Stat. L., 329)—An Act Relating to leases on the Hot Springs Reservation, and for other purposes.

Secretary of the Interior granted discretionary power for granting of leases and privileges.

1898—Act of May 9, 1898 (30 Stat. L., 403)—An Act Authorizing the Supreme Lodge of the Knights of Pythias to erect and maintain a sanitarium and bathhouse on the Government reservation, at the city of Hot Springs, Arkansas.

Rights granted to continue for not to exceed ninety-nine years subject to certain conditions, non-fulfillment of which cause forfeiture to the Government.

1900—Act of February 10, 1900 (31 Stat. L., 28)—An Act To amend section 4 of the Act of Congress approved June 16, 1880, granting to the city of Hot Springs, Arkansas, certain lands as a city park, and for other purposes.

Original grant made more liberal provided municipality relinquishes title to a lot desired by Government for administrative purposes.

1900—Act of March 26, 1900 (31 Stat. L., 51)—An Act To extend the time for the completion of the incline railway on West Mountain, Hot Springs Reservation.

A further extension of three years granted.

1901—Act of March 3, 1901 (31 Stat. L., 1133, 1188)—An Act Making appropriations for sundry civil expenses of the Government for the fiscal year ending June thirtieth, nineteen hundred and two, and for other purposes.

Payment of certain claims for value of condemned houses on reservation after investigation made authorized.

LAWS 127

1903—Act of January 30, 1903 (32 Stat. L., 788)—An Act To extend the time for the completion on the incline railway on West Mountain, Hot Springs, Reservation.

> Extension of one year granted.

1904—Act of April 12, 1904 (33 Stat. L., 173)—An Act To amend an act approved December 16, 1878, and to authorize the Secretary of the Interior to grant additional water rights to hotels and bathhouses at Hot Springs, Arkansas, and for other purposes.

> Restriction to specified number of tubs as provided by previous act done away with and authority given Secretary of the Interior to grant privileges for as many tubs as he deems proper and hot water will justify.

1904—Act of April 20, 1904 (33 Stat. L., 187)—An Act Conferring jurisdiction upon United States Commissioners over offenses committed in a portion of the permanent Hot Springs Mountain Reservation, Arkansas.

> Acceptance of jurisdiction conferred by Arkansas legislature by the act of February 21, 1903, reserving taxing and process rights to State. The act further places the reservation within the federal district for Eastern Arkansas; prescribes punishments for offenses, including the illegal prescribing and using of the waters; defines the powers of United States commissioners; and provides rules regarding issue of process by commissioners, etc.

1906—Act of May 23, 1906 (34 Stat. L., 198)—An Act To change the line of the reservation at Hot Springs, Arkansas, and of Reserve Avenue.

1907—Act of March 2, 1907 (34 Stat. L., 1218)—An Act To amend an Act entitled "An Act conferring jurisdiction upon United States commissioners over offenses committed in a portion of the permanent Hot Springs Mountain Reservation, Arkansas," approved April 20, 1904.

Clarifies the phraseology of the act of April 20, 1904.

1908—Act of April 30, 1908 (35 Stat. L., 98)—An Act To confer title in fee and to authorize the disposition of certain lots now situate on Hot Springs Reservation, in the State of Arkansas, and for other purposes.

Grants certain lots on Hot Springs Reservation to school district of Hot Springs and repeals all laws or parts of laws in conflict therewith.

1910—Act of March 12, 1910 (36 Stat. L., 235)—An Act Granting unto the Hot Springs Street Railway Company, its successors and assigns, the right to maintain and operate its electric railway along the Northern border of that portion of the Hot Springs Reservation, in the State of Arkansas, known as the Whittington Lake Reserve Park.

Grants right of way during existence of franchise granted by city of Hot Springs, and reserves right to alter, amend, or repeal.

1910—Act of June 25, 1910 (36 Stat. L., 844)—An Act Granting to the city of Hot Springs, Arkansas, land for street purposes.

1911—Act of Feb. 15, 1911 (36 Stat. L., 906)—An Act Authorizing the Hot Springs Lodge, numbered sixty-two, Ancient Free and Accepted Masons, under the jurisdiction of the Grand Lodge of Arkansas, to occupy and construct buildings for the use of the organization on lots numbered 1 and 2, in block numbered 114, in the city of Hot Springs, Arkansas.

Lots granted for the erection of a Masonic home, to be completed in five years. Lots to revert to Government if home not built in five years or if any other use ever made of premises than one originally contemplated.

1911—Act of March 2, 1911 (36 Stat. L., 1015)—An Act

LAWS 129

> Limiting the privileges of the Government free bathhouse on the public reservation at Hot Springs, Arkansas, to persons who are without and unable to obtain the means to pay for baths.

Requires an oath as to indigency and provides penalty for false swearing.

1911—Act of March 3, 1911 (36 Stat. L., 1086)—An Act To amend section one of the act approved March 2, 1907, being an act to amend an Act entitled "An Act Conferring jurisdiction upon United States Commissioners over offenses committed on a portion of the permanent Hot Springs Mountain Reservation, Arkansas."

Amends Sec. 1 of the Act of March 2, 1907 to read as follows: That any United States Commissioner duly appointed by the United States district court for the eastern district of Arkansas, and residing in said district, shall have power and jurisdiction to hear and act upon all complaints made of any and all violations of said Act of Congress approved April twentieth, nineteen hundred and four.

1912—Act of June 3, 1912 (37 Stat. L., 121)—An Act Authorizing the Leo N. Levi Memorial Hospital Association to occupy and construct buildings for the use of the corporation in lots numbered 3 and 4, block numbered 114, in the city of Hot Springs, Arkansas.

Similar to Masonic grant, supra.

1912—Act of August 21, 1912 (37 Stat. L., 322)—An Act Authorizing the city of Hot Springs, Arkansas, to occupy and construct buildings for the use of the fire department of said city on lot numbered 3, block numbered 115, in the city of Hot Springs, Arkansas.

Similar to Masonic grant, supra.

1912—Act of August 24, 1912 (37 Stat. L., 457)—An Act Making appropriations for sundry civil expenses of the Government for the fiscal year ending June thirtieth, nineteen hundred and thirteen, and for other purposes.

Authorizes and directs Secretary of the Interior to make a survey of the sewer system of the city of Hot Springs abutting the Hot Springs Reservation, Arkansas.

Authorizes Secretary of Interior to lease Arlington Hotel property in Hot Springs for not to exceed twenty years, and makes provision as to valuation of improvements made by lessee under expiring lease.

1916—Act of July 8, 1916 (39 Stat. L., 351)—An Act Authorizing the Secretary of the Interior to furnish hot water from the hot springs on the Hot Springs Reservation for drinking and bathing purposes free of cost to the Leo N. Levi Memorial Hospital Association.

Authorization made subject to proviso that hospital accept and treat emergency patients free of charge.

1920—Act of June 5, 1920 (41 Stat. L., 918)—An Act Making appropriations for sundry civil expenses of the Government for the fiscal year ending June thirtieth, nineteen hundred and twenty-one, and for other purposes.

Unexpended balance of appropriation for fiscal year 1919 reappropriated and made available for fiscal year 1921; and Secretary of the Interior authorized to expend same for buildings and to accept sites which may be donated for same in city of Hot Springs. The Secretary also authorized to charge physicians, masseurs and bath attendants prescribing or using waters from the reservation fees for the exercise of those privileges.

1921—Act of March 4, 1921 (41 Stat. L., 1407)—An Act Making appropriations for sundry civil expenses of the Government for the fiscal year ending June thirtieth, nineteen hundred and twenty-one, and for other purposes.

* * * *

Hereafter the Hot Springs Reservation shall be known as the Hot Springs National Park.

APPENDIX 5

FINANCIAL STATEMENTS

Explanatory Note

Statements showing appropriations, receipts, expenditures and other financial data for a series of years constitute the most effective single means of exhibiting the growth and development of a service. Due to the fact that Congress has adopted no uniform plan of appropriation for the several services and the latter employ no uniform plan in respect to the recording and reporting of their receipts and expenditures, it is impossible to present data of this character according to any standard scheme of presentation. In the case of some services the administrative reports contain tables showing financial conditions and operations of the service in considerable detail; in others financial data are almost wholly lacking. Careful study has in all cases been made of such data as are available, and the effort has been made to present the results in such a form as will exhibit the financial operations of the services in the most effective way that circumstances permit.

Under the organic act establishing most of the parks the Department of the Interior had authority to expend the revenues of these parks in the discretion of the Secretary or his duly authorized representative. Since 1918 the revenues of all the parks, with the exception of Hot Springs have been covered into the Treasury, and no expenditures of these amounts have been made without the authorization of Congress. Up to and including 1918 the appropriations to the parks were made under the Department of the Interior and the War Department. Since that date all appropriations have been made under the Department of the Interior with the exception of Sullys Hill Park which receives appropriations under the Department of Agriculture. In addition the National Park Service benefits from the appropriation to the Department of the Interior for "contingent expenses" of the department.

In the table immediately following the "appropriations to the national parks" include only the regular appropriations made by Congress, but do not include the revenues of the parks. No account is taken of certified claims which are generally small. In the statement showing expenditures the items are figured on the accrual basis, with the exception of 1920 which is figured on the cash basis, and include the amounts spent out of the revenues and out of the regular appropriations of the parks. The item "additional compensation" includes the bonus received by the National Park Service in Washington and in the field.

FINANCIAL STATEMENTS

NATIONAL PARK SERVICE
*Appropriations, ** Revenues, and * Expenditures; Fiscal Years 1917–1919, Inclusive

Object	1917 Appropriation	1917 Revenues	1917 b Expenditure	1918 Appropriation	1918 Revenues	1918 b Expenditure	1919 Appropriation	1919 Expenditure
National Park Service	$ 3,666.67	....	$ 2,513.62	$ 17,600.00	....	$ 17,413.33	$ 19,200.00	$ 19,177.50
Additional Compensation	....	....	....	17,413.33	....	17,413.33	17,041.60	17,041.60
Yellowstone National Park, Wyo.	205,700.00	54,795.69	248,765.61	e 178,000.00	71,393.56	273,552.41	d 334,920.00	330,034.19
Yosemite National Park, Calif.	250,000.00	53,500.66	305,085.90	235,000.00	65,865.65	315,343.91	255,000.00	254,295.44
Glacier National Park, Mont.	110,000.00	3,202.40	108,000.91	115,000.00	4,438.22	131,889.68	80,000.00	81,450.18
Sequoia National Park, Calif.	72,300.00	10,326.60	66,020.32	25,000.00	13,402.53	50,187.16	30,510.00	30,417.48
General Grant National Park, Calif.	2,000.00	1,153.78	2,536.52	2,000.00	1,801.63	5,951.85	4,500.00	4,481.90
Mount Rainier National Park, Wash.	30,000.00	14,346.80	46,116.23	75,000.00	17,241.25	109,562.63	24,600.00	24,552.28
Crater Lake National Park, Ore.	58,000.00	e 4,565.25	39,053.10	51,500.00	e 4,005.72	64,578.88	13,225.00	13,204.82
Wind Cave National Park, S. Dak.	2,500.00	1,632.60	3,512.91	2,500.00	4,082.60	10,506.53	4,000.00	3,988.52
Mesa Verde National Park, Colo.	10,000.00	c 130.14	9,999.00	10,000.00	e 2,763.75	9,913.00	18,000.00	17,022.44
Platt National Park, Okla.	8,000.00	434.11	8,434.11	7,180.00	1,010.04	8,879.72	7,500.00	7,483.65
f Sullys Hill Park, N. Dak.	5,000.00	....	5,000.00	5,000.00	....	5,000.00	5,000.00	5,000.00
Rocky Mountain National Park, Colo.	10,000.00	e 871.27	9,964.24	10,000.00	e 598.75	9,922.10	10,000.00	9,994.36
Hawaii National Park	....	....	....	....	....	....	750.00	730.50
Lassen Volcanic National Park, Cal.	....	e 81.25	....	....	e 118.05	....	....	....
Mount McKinley National Park, Alaska	....	....	....	....	....	....	....	....
Grand Canyon National Park, Arizona	....	....	....	....	....	....	....	....
Lafayette National Park, Maine	....	....	14,963.81	....	....	....	....	....
Zion National Park, Utah	15,000.00	35,611.75	31,302.98	....	28,833.44	42,822.02	g 190,000.00	b 90,790.72
Hot Springs National Park, Ark.	....	....	....	....	....	....	....	....
National Monuments, General	3,500.00	....	2,586.66	5,000.00	e 225.00	4,832.70	10,000.00	9,496.00

133

*Appropriations, ** Revenues, and * Expenditures; Fiscal Years 1917-1919, Inclusive—(Continued)

Object	ᵃ 1917			ᵃ 1918			1919	
	Appropriation	Revenues ᶠ	ᵇ Expenditure	Appropriation	Revenues	ᵇ Expenditure	Appropriation	Expenditure
Navajo National Monument, Arizona	3,000.00	....	ʰ 1,962.69	....	....	....	....	....
Mukuntuweap National Monument, Utah	15,000.00	....	14,963.81	....	....	....	....	....
Sieur de Monts National Monument, Maine	....	....	....	....	....	....	10,000.00	9,972.42
Totals	803,666.67	180,652.30	920,782.42	756,193.33	215,780.19	1,077,769.25	1,034,246.60	929,136.00

* Data from Treasury's Combined Statement.
** Data from Annual Reports, Department of Interior.
ᵃ Includes amounts appropriated under the Departments of War and Interior.
ᵇ Includes expenditures out of the revenues of the parks.
ᶜ Unexpended balance of War Department, $3259.48, made available for 1919 under the Department of Interior.
ᵈ Includes repayment on account of expenditures for fighting forest fires and for repairs on account of other damages.
ᵉ Expenditure of revenues not authorized by statute.
ᶠ No year appropriation; under Department of Agriculture.
ᵍ Includes $50,000 appropriated out of the revenues of the park.
ʰ Expended under the direction of the Smithsonian Institute.

FINANCIAL STATEMENTS

NATIONAL PARK SERVICE
*Appropriations and Expenditures: Fiscal Years 1920 to 1922, Inclusive

Object	1920 Appropriation	1920 Expenditure	1921 Appropriation	1921 Expenditure	1922 Appropriation	1922 Expenditure
National Park Service	22,220.00	21,524.46	27,420.65		a 56,020.00	
Additional Compensation	44,386.75	44,386.75	51,370.65			
Yellowstone National Park, Wyo.	b 326,526.64	325,838.36	b 286,500.00		350,000.00	
Yosemite National Park, Calif.	200,000.00	199,973.96	b 303,000.00		300,000.00	
Glacier National Park, Mont.	166,849.12	168,349.12	b 107,564.09		195,000.00	
Sequoia National Park, Calif.	35,000.00	34,846.82	36,000.00		86,000.00	
General Grant National Park, Calif.	6,000.00	5,992.89	5,300.00		6,000.00	
Mount Rainier National Park, Wash.	32,500.00	32,409.56	40,000.00		150,000.00	
Crater Lake National Park, Ore.	28,225.00	28,170.53	25,300.00		25,300.00	
Wind Cave National Park, S. Dak.	4,000.00	3,986.48	5,000.00		7,500.00	
Mesa Verde National Park, Colo.	11,000.00	10,959.69	14,000.00		16,400.00	
Platt National Park, Okla.	6,000.00	5,980.04	9,000.00		7,500.00	
f Sullys Hill Park, N. Dak.	5,000.00	5,000.00	5,000.00		75,000.00	
Rocky Mountain National Park, Colo.	10,000.00	9,914.74	40,000.00		65,000.00	
Hawaii National Park	750.00	747.52	1,000.00		10,000.00	
Lassen Volcanic National Park, Calif.			2,500.00		3,000.00	
Mount McKinley National Park, Alaska					8,000.00	
Grand Canyon National Park, Arizona	40,000.00	40,000.00	60,000.00		100,000.00	
Lafayette National Park, Maine	10,000.00	9,919.74	20,000.00		25,000.00	
Zion National Park, Utah			8,885.07		10,000.00	
Hot Springs National Park, Ark.	c	d 64,922.69	e 85,000.00			
National Monuments, General	8,000.00		8,000.00		12,500.00	
Navajo National Monument, Arizona						
Mukuntuweap National Monument, Utah						
Sieur de Monte National Monument, Maine						
	956,457.51	1,012,923.29	1,140,839.81		1,508,220.00	

* Data from Treasury's Combined Statement.
a Includes $25,000 for fighting forest fires in National Parks.
b Included repayments on account of expenditures for fighting forest fires and for repairs on account of other damages.
c Unexpended balance made available in 1920 and again in 1921.
d Includes $35,710.33 spent out of the revenues of the park.
e Includes $25,000 appropriated out of the revenues of the park.
f No year appropriation; under Department of Agriculture.

NATIONAL PARK SERVICE

Total* Appropriations Received by the National Parks up to and Including 1922

Name of Park	Department Under Which Appropriated			Total
	Interior	[a] War	Agriculture	
[b] National Park Service	276,348.97			276,348.97
Yellowstone National Park	1,679,954.62	3,163,095.86		4,843,050.48
Yosemite National Park	2,192,599.25			2,192,599.25
Glacier National Park	1,183,613.21			1,183,613.21
Sequoia National Park	494,849.69			494,849.69
General Grant National Park	59,358.65			59,358.65
Mount Rainier National Park	496,000.00	240,000.00		736,000.00
Crater Lake National Park	173,945.00	370,306.98		544,251.98
Wind Cave National Park	57,400.00		26,000.00	83,400.00
Mesa Verde National Park	176,400.00			176,400.00
Platt National Park	119,680.00			119,680.00
Sullys Hill Park	500.00		52,000.00	52,500.00
Rocky Mountain National Park	156,000.00			156,000.00
Hawaii National Park	12,500.00			12,500.00
Lassen Volcanic National Park	5,500.00			5,500.00
Mount McKinley National Park	8,000.00			8,000.00
Grand Canyon National Park	200,000.00			200,000.00
Lafayette National Park	45,000.00			45,000.00
Zion National Park	18,885.07			18,885.07
Hot Springs National Park	[c] 732,244.30			732,244.30
National Monuments, general	47,451.85			47,451.85
Navajo National Monument	3,000.00			3,000.00
Mukuntuweap National Monument	15,000.00			15,000.00
Sieur de Monts National Monument	10,000.00			10,000.00
Total	8,164,230.61	3,773,402.84	78,000.00	12,015,633.45

* Data up to and including 1918 from National Park Service "Statement of Appropriations 1879 to 1918, Inclusive."
* Data 1919 to 1922 inclusive from Digest of Appropriations.
[a] Since 1918 all appropriations except Sullys Hill Park have been under the Department of Interior.
[b] Includes $130,222.30 "Additional Compensation" received by the service in Washington and in the field.
[c] Of this amount $160,744.78 was appropriated out of the revenues of the parks.

STATISTICS OF VISITORS

Visitors to the National Parks, 1908-1920

Name	1908	1909	1910	1911	1912	1913	1914
Hot Springs National Park	(1)	(1)	2 120,000	2 130,000	2 135,000	2 135,000	2 125,000
Yellowstone National Park	19,542	32,545	19,575	23,054	22,970	24,929	20,250
Sequoia National Park	1,251	854	2,407	3,114	2,923	3,823	4,667
Yosemite National Park	8,850	13,182	13,619	12,530	10,884	13,735	15,145
General Grant National Park	1,773	798	1,178	2,160	2,240	2,756	3,735
Mount Rainier National Park	2,826	5,968	8,000	10,306	8,946	13,501	15,038
Crater Lake National Park	5,275	4,171	2 5,000	2 4,500	5,235	6,253	7,996
Wind Cave National Park	3,171	3,216	3,387	3,887	3,199	3,988	3,592
Platt National Park	2 26,000	2 25,000	2 25,000	2 30,000	2 31,000	2 35,000	2 30,000
Sullys Hill National Park	2 250	2 190	2 190	2 200	2 200	2 300	2 500
Mesa Verde National Park	2 80	165	250	206	230	282	502
Glacier National Park				2 4,000	6,257	12,138	14,168
Rocky Mountain National Park							
Hawaii National Park							
Lassen Volcanic National Park							
Mount McKinley National Park							
Grand Canyon National Park							
Lafayette National Park							
Zion National Park							
Total	69,018	86,089	198,606	223,957	229,084	251,703	235,193

Visitors to the National Parks, 1908-1920—Continued

Name of park	1915	1916	1917	1918	1919	1920	1921
Hot Springs National Park	b 115,000	b 118,740	b 135,000	b 140,000	b 160,490	b 162,850	b 130,968
Yellowstone National Park	51,895	35,849	35,400	21,275	62,261	79,777	81,651
Sequoia National Park	7,647	10,780	18,510	15,001	30,443	31,508	28,263
Yosemite National Park	33,452	33,390	34,510	33,497	58,362	68,906	91,513
General Grant National Park	10,523	15,360	17,390	15,496	21,574	19,661	30,312
Mount Rainier National Park	35,166	23,989	35,568	43,901	55,232	56,491	55,771
Crater Lake National Park	11,371	12,265	11,645	13,231	16,645	20,135	28,617
Wind Cave National Park	2,817	b 9,000	16,742	14,431	26,312	27,023	28,336
Platt National Park	b 20,000	b 30,000	b 35,000	b 36,000	b 25,000	b 38,000	b 60,000
Sullys Hill Park	b 1,000	b 1,500	2,207	4,188	4,026	9,341	9,100
Mesa Verde National Park	14,265	12,839	18,387	9,086	18,956	22,449	19,736
Rocky Mountain National Park	663	1,385	2,223	2,058	2,287	2,890	3,003
Glacier National Park	b 31,000	b 51,000	b 117,186	b 101,497	b 169,492	b 240,906	273,737
Hawaii National Park	....	(a)	(a)	(a)	(a)	(a)	b 16,071
Lassen Volcanic National Park	....	(a)	b 8,500	b 2,000	b 2,500	b 2,000	b 10,000
Mount McKinley National Park	....	....	(a)	(a)	(a)	(a)	(a)
Grand Canyon National Park	....	....	....	....	37,745	67,315	b 67,485
Lafayette National Park	....	....	....	....	b 64,000	b 66,500	b 69,836
Zion National Park	....	....	....	....	....	3,092	2,937
Total	334,799	356,097	488,268	451,661	755,325	919,504	1,007,335

a No record.   b Estimated.

Visitors to Some of the National Monuments in 1919–20 [a]

Name	1919	1920	1921
Capulin Mountain, New Mexico	b 1,500	b 3,200	b 3,000
Casa Grande, Arizona	3,677	7,720	6,296
Colorado, Colorado	3,000	b 1,200	b 5,500
Devils Tower, Wyoming			b 7,000
El Morro, New Mexico		b 2,000	b 3,000
Montezuma Castle, Arizona		b 2,500	b 4,500
Muir Woods, California	b 43,200	b 77,577	b 87,400
Navajo, Arizona		64	65
Papago Saguaro, Arizona		b 5,000	b 3,000
Petrified Forest, Arizona	b 3,000	b 30,390	b 32,700
Scotts Bluff, Nebraska		b 5,000	b 6,000
Tumacacori, Arizona		b 4,300	b 5,000
Verendrye, North Dakota			b 1,000
Zion, Utah [c]	1,814		
Total	56,191	138,951	164,461

[a] No records for other 13 National monuments.
[b] Estimated.
[c] Created a national park Nov. 19, 1919.

APPENDIX 7

BIBLIOGRAPHY [1]

Explanatory Note

The bibliographies appended to the several monographs aim to list only those works which deal directly with the services to which they relate, their history, activities, organization, methods of business, problems, etc. They are intended primarily to meet the needs of those persons who desire to make a further study of the services from an administrative standpoint. They thus do not include the titles of publications of the services themselves, except in so far as they treat of the services, their work and problems. Nor do they include books or articles dealing merely with technical features other than administrative of the work of the services. In a few cases explanatory notes have been appended where it was thought they would aid in making known the character or value of the publication to which they relate.

After the completion of the series, the bibliographies may be assembled and separately published as a bibliography of the Administrative Branch of the National Government.

Bibliographies

U. S. *Dept. of the interior.* Government publications on . . . national parks [Washington, Govt. print. off., 1916—
  A two-page list of goverment publications has been

[1] Compiled by M. Alice Matthews.

issued (1916) for each of the following national parks: Crater Lake, Glacier, Mesa Verde, Mount Rainier, Rocky Mountain, Sequoia and General Grant, Yellowstone and the Yosemite. These lists are issued primarily for distribution to tourists in the parks.

───── ───── List of national park publications. [Washington, Govt. print. off., 1912] 27 p. incl. map.

Bibliography of each park is in 3 sections: government publications; books; magazine articles.

───── ───── Magazine articles on national parks, reservations and monuments. [Washington, Govt. print. off., 1911] 15 p.

───── ───── National park publications. (*In its* Progress in the development of the national parks . . . Washington, Govt. print. off., 1916. p. 36-9)

───── *National park service.* Bibliography of books and magazine articles on national park subjects. (*In its* Report, 1917, p. 231-49; 1918, p. 249-60; 1919, p. 335-47)

───── ───── National park publications. (*In its* Report, 1920. pp. 394-99)

───── *Superintendent of documents.* Geography and explorations, natural wonders, scenery and national parks: list of publications relating to above subjects for sale by Superintendent of documents. Washington, Govt. print. off., 1921. 19 p. (Price list 35, 6th ed.)

OFFICIAL PUBLICATIONS

Uniform rules and regulations prescribed by the Secretaries of the interior, agriculture, and war to carry out the provisions of the "Act for the preservation of American antiquities," approved June 8, 1906. [Washington, Govt. print. off., 1906] 3 p.

U. S. *Biological survey.* National reservation for the protection of wild life. By T. S. Palmer. [Washington, Govt. print off., 1912] 32 p. (*Its* Circular no. 87)

BIBLIOGRAPHY

"Of the 16 national parks, 10 may properly be considered game refuges."
Bibliography: National game preserves and other refuges; National bird reservations, pp. 21-9.

—— —— Report of the chief of the Bureau of biological survey, 1906—Washington, Govt. print. off., 1907——

[Contains annual review of the progress of game protection in the national parks and elsewhere]

—— *Bureau of fisheries.* Report of the commissioner. . . . Washington, Govt. print. off., 1873——
The Bureau of fisheries coöperates in stocking the streams and lakes in the national parks. Fish hatcheries are maintained in some of them.

——*Congress. House. Committee on appropriations.* Sundry civil appropriation bill, 1922. Hearings . . . Washington, Govt. print. off., 1920.
"National park service," pp. 1928-2058.

—— —— —— *Committee on military affairs.* Mammoth Cave national park. Hearing . . . on H. R. 1666, establishing the Mammoth Cave national park [Feb. 1, 1912] Washington, Govt. print. off., 1912. 26 p.

—— —— *Committee on public lands.* [Hearings and reports, arranged chronologically]

—— —— —— Hearings. . . . January 11, 1905, for preservation of prehistoric ruins on the public lands. Creation of the Pajarito cliff dwellers national park in New Mexico and the Mesa Verde national park in Colorado, also full text of each bill as reported by the Committee, the same being S. 5603, H. R. 7269 and 5986. . . . Washington, Govt. print. off., 1905. 39 p.

—— —— —— Prehistoric ruins on public lands. Report to accompany S. 5603 [for preservation of historic and prehistoric ruins, monuments, archaeological objects and other antiquities] Jan. 19, 1905. Washington, Govt. print. off.,

1905. 10 p. (58th Cong., 3d sess. House. Rept. 3704)
Serial 4761
To authorize Secretary of the interior to make temporary withdrawal of land containing such ruins . . . and to have care and custody of same. Bibliography: p. 8-10.

———— ———— ———— Preservation of American antiquities. Report to accompany H. R. 11016. Mar. 12, 1906. [Washington, Govt. print. off., 1906] 8 p. (59th Cong., 1st sess. House. Rept. 2224) Serial 4906

[Contains a list of ruins grouped in various districts, which were thought of sufficient historic and scientific interest and scenic beauty to warrant their organization into permanent national parks]

———— ———— ———— . . . Glacier national park . . . Report [To accompany S. 5648] [Washington, Govt. print. off., 1909] 6 p. (60th Cong., 2d sess. House. Rept. 2100)
Serial 5384.

———— ———— ———— San Francisco and Hetch Hetchy reservoir, hearings Jan. 9—[21] 1909, on H. J. R. 223 [to allow city and county of San Francisco to exchange lands for reservoir sites in Lake Eleanor and Hetch Hetchy valleys in Yosemite national park, etc.] Washington, Govt. print. off., 1909. 426 p.

———— ———— ———— . . . Glacier national park, Mont. . . . Report. [To accompany S. 2777] . . . [Washington, Govt. print. off., 1910] 6 p. (61st Cong., 2d sess. House. Rept. 767) Serial 5592.

———— ———— ———— . . . Glacier national park, Mont. . . . Report. [To accompany H. R. 1679] [Washington, Govt. print. off., 1912] 11 p. (62d Cong., 2d sess. House. Rept. 812) Serial 6132.

———— ———— ———— Establishment of a National park service. Hearing . . . on H. R. 22995, a bill to establish a national park service, and for other purposes, Wednesday, April 24, 1912. Washington, Govt. print. off., 1912. 34 p.

———— ———— ———— Tioga road in Yosemite national park.

Hearings before the subcommittee. . . . March 18, 1912, on H. R. 21718 and 21719. Statements by Hon. John B. Curtin . . . and Mr. Aldis B. Browne . . . Washington, Govt. print. off., 1912. 19 p.

────── ────── ────── Western boundary of Yosemite national park. Hearings . . . March 20, 1912 on H. R. 21954. Statement of Hon. John B. Curtin, of Sonora, Cal. Washington, Govt. print. off., 1912. 13 p.

────── ────── ────── Yosemite national park. Hearing on 21535 . . . March 20, 1912. [Washington, Govt. print. off., 1912] 6 p.

────── ────── ────── National park service. Hearing . . . on H. R. 104, a bill to establish a National park service and for other purposes. April 29, 1914. Washington, Govt. print. off., 1914. 81 p.

────── ────── ────── Rocky Mountain national park. Hearing . . . on S. 6309, a bill to establish the Rocky Mountain national park in the State of Colorado, and for other purposes. Washington, Govt. print. off., 1915. 75 p.

────── ────── ────── . . . Rocky Mountain national park, Colorado . . . Report. [To accompany S. 6309] [Washington, Govt. print. off., 1915] 48 p. (63d Cong., 3d sess. House. Rept. 1275) Serial 6766

────── ────── ────── . . . Lassen volcanic national park . . . Report. [To accompany H. R. 348] [Washington, Govt. print. off., 1916] 24 p. (64th Cong., 1st sess. House. Rept. 749) Serial 6905

────── ────── ────── National park in the territory of Hawaii. Hearing . . . on H. R. 9525 . . . Feb. 3, 1916. Washington, Govt. print. off., 1916. 30 p.

────── ────── ────── National park service. Hearing . . . on H. R. 434 and H. R. 8668, bills to establish a national park service and for other purposes, April 5 and 6, 1916. Washington, Govt. print. off., 1916. 186 p.

────── ────── ────── . . . National park service. . . . Report [To accompany H. R. 15522] [Washington, Govt. print.

off., 1916] 7 p. (64th Cong., 1st sess. House. Rept. 700)
Serial 6904

————— ————— ————— Mt. Baker national park, Washington. Report to accompany H. R. 9805. [Washington, Govt. print. off., 1917] 8 p. (64th Cong., 2d sess. House. Rept. 1372)
Serial 7110

————— ————— ————— Mt. McKinley national park, Alaska. Report to accompany S. 5716. [Washington, Govt. print. off., 1917] 2 p. (64th Cong., 2d sess. House. Rept. 1273).
Serial 7110

————— ————— ————— Sawtooth national park, Idaho. Report to accompany H. R. 6799. Washington, Govt. print. off., 1917. 11 p. plates. (64th Cong., 2d sess. House. Rept. 1356)
Serial 7110

————— ————— ————— Grand Canyon national park. Report to accompany S. 390, Oct. 18, 1918. Washington, Govt. print. off., 1918. 10 p. (65th Cong., 2d sess. House. Rept 832)
Serial 7308

————— ————— ————— Change name of Sequoia national park to Roosevelt national park. Report to accompany S. 2021. [Washington, Govt. print. off., 1919] 6, 7 p. (65th Cong., 3d sess. House. Rept. 1063)
Serial 7455

————— ————— ————— Lafayette national park. Report to accompany S. 4957. [Washington, Govt. print. off., 1919] 5 p. (66th Cong., 3d sess. House. Rept. 932)
Serial 7454

————— ————— ————— Zion national park. Report to accompany S. 425. [Washington, Govt. print. off., 1919] 3 p. (66th Cong., 1st sess. House. Rept. 262)
Serial 7593

————— ————— ————— National redwood park. Report to accompany H. Res. 159. [Washington, Govt. print. off., 1920] 2 p. (66th Cong., 2d sess. House. Rept. 871)
Serial 7656

————— ————— *Senate. Committee on public lands. . . .* Preservation of historic and prehistoric ruins, etc. Hearings before the subcommittee of the Committee on public lands . . . consisting of Senators Fulton (chairman),

BIBLIOGRAPHY

Bard, and Newlands, on the bill (S. 4127) . . . and the bill (S. 5603) . . . April 28, 1904—Washington, Govt. print. off., 1904. 30 p. (58th Cong., 2d sess. Senate. Doc. no. 314) Serial 4592

——— ——— ——— . . . To establish Glacier national park in Montana . . . Report. [To accompany S. 5648] [Washington, Govt. print. off., 1908] 5 p. plates, fold. map. (60th Cong., 1st sess. Senate. Rept. 580)
  Serial 5219

——— ——— ——— Hetch Hetchy reservoir site, Hearing [Feb. 10, 12, 1909] on S. J. R. 123, to allow city and county of San Francisco to exchange lands for reservoir sites in Lake Eleanor and Hetch Hetchy valleys in Yosemite national park [etc.] Washington, Govt. print. off., 1909. 160 p.

——— ——— ——— . . . Glacier national park in Montana . . . Report. [To accompany S. 2777] . . . [Washington, Govt. print. off., 1910] 5 p. 10 pl., fold, map. (61st Cong., 2d sess. Senate. Rept. 106) Serial 5582

——— ——— ——— Bureau of national parks. Hearing . . . on S. 3463, a bill to establish a bureau of national parks and for other purposes. April 17, 1912. . . . Washington, Govt. print. off., 1912. 9 p.

[Statement of Walter L. Fisher, Secretary of the Interior]

——— ——— ——— Bureau of national parks. Report. To accompany S. 3463. [Washington, Govt. print. off., 1912] 6 p. (62d Cong., 2d sess. Senate. Rept. 676)
  Serial 6121

——— ——— ——— . . . Lassen volcanic national park. . . . Report. [To accompany H. R. 348] [Washington, Govt. print. off., 1916] 23 p. (64th Cong., 1st sess. Senate. Rept. 536) Serial 6899
Appended is House report no. 749, 64th Cong., 1st sess. Report to accompany H. R. 348.

——— ——— ——— . . . National park service. . . . Report.

THE NATIONAL PARK SERVICE

[To accompany H. R. 15522] [Washington, Govt. print. off., 1916] 4 p. (64th Cong., 1st sess. Senate. Rept. 662) Serial 6899

────── ────── ────── Grand Canyon national park, Arizona. Report to accompany S. 8250. [Washington, Govt. print. off., 1917] 3 p. (64th Cong., 2d sess. Senate. Rept. 1082) Serial 7106

────── ────── ────── Grand Canyon national park. Report to accompany S. 390. . . . [Washington, Govt. print off., 1918] 3 p. (65th Cong., 2d sess. Senate. Rept. 321) Serial 7304

────── ────── ────── Lafayette national park. Report to accompany S. 4957. [Washington, Govt. print. off., 1918] 1 p. (65th Cong., 2d sess. Senate. Rept. 576) Serial 7304

────── ────── ────── Mount Desert national park, Me. Report to accompany S. 4569. [Washington, Govt. print. off., 1918] 2 p. (65th Cong., 2d sess. Senate. Rept. 503) Serial 7304

────── ────── ────── Sequoia national park. Report to accompany S. 2021. [Washington, Govt. print. off., 1919] 4 p. (65th Cong., 3d sess. Senate. Rept. 647) Serial 7452

────── ────── ────── Zion national park, Utah. Report to accompany S. 425. [Washington, Govt. print. off., 1919] 2 p. (66th Cong., 1st sess. Senate. Rept. 22) Serial 7590

────── ────── ────── Acceptance of cession of jurisdiction of Yosemite, Sequoia, and General Grant national parks, Calif. Report to accompany H. R. 12044. Washington, Govt. print. off., 1920. 1 p. (66th Cong., 2d sess. Senate. Rept. 590) Serial 7649

────── ────── ────── Roosevelt national park. Report to accompany S. 1391. Washington, Govt. print. off., 1920. 4 p. (66th Cong., 2d sess. Senate. Rept. 452) Serial 7649

────── *Dept. of the interior.* [Publications relating to national parks in general]

BIBLIOGRAPHY 149

———— ————Annual reports of the Department of the interior . . . [with accompanying documents] Washington, Govt. print. off., [etc.] 1849-19—plates, ports, maps (part fold.) fold. plans, fold. tables.

Up to 1915 these reports included the annual reports of the superintendents of the various parks. In 1915 the report of the General superintendent and landscape engineer preceded the reports of the superintendents. In 1916, excerpts from reports of supervisors of national parks were printed with the first annual report of the Superintendent of national parks.

———— ———— Annual report of the Superintendent of national parks to the Secretary of the interior for the fiscal year ended June 30, 1916. Washington, Govt. print. off., 1916. 89 p.

[The Superintendent of national parks was the successor of the General superintendent and landscape engineer of national parks]

———— ———— Improvement and management of national parks. Letter from the Secretary of the treasury, transmitting a copy of a communication from the Secretary of the interior relating to the administration of the appropriations for the improvement and management of national parks, and submitting an item of legislation relating thereto. [Washington, Govt. print. off., 1916] 22 p. incl. tables. (64th Cong., 1st sess. House. Doc. 515)   Serial 7098

National park conference, 1st, Yellowstone national park, Sept. 11-12, 1911. Proceedings of the first National park conference . . . Washington, Govt. print. off., 1912. 209 p.

[This conference was called by Walter L. Fisher, Secretary of the interior, and was made up of departmental officials, superintendents of parks, representatives of railroads, and others. Ways were sought of improving and popularizing the great playgrounds of America. As a result of the conference numerous illustrated pamphlets were published]

National park conference, 2d, Yosemite national park, Oct. 14-16, 1912. Proceedings of the second National park conference . . . Washington, Govt. print. off., 1913. 144 p.

[Consists mainly of a discussion regarding the advisability of admitting automobiles to the national parks]

National park conference, 3d, Berkeley, Cal., Mar. 11-13, 1915. Proceedings of the third National park conference. . . . Washington, Govt. print. off., 1915. 166 p.

Discussion of national park problems by officers of the government and others.

National park conference, 4th, Washington, D. C., Jan. 2-6, 1917. Proceedings of the fourth National park conference. . . . Washington, Govt. print. off., 1917. 100 (?) p.

—— —— National park pictures collected and exhibited by the Department of the interior. [Washington, Govt. print. off., 1911] 15 p.

"This collection of pictures has been assembled for free exhibition at public libraries and other institutions." *cf.* p. 1.

—— —— National park service in the District of Columbia . . . communication from the Secretary of the interior submitting an estimate of appropriations for the administration in the District of Columbia of the National park service created by the act of Congress, approved Aug. 25, 1916. Washington, Govt. print. off., 1916. 2 p. (64th Cong., 1st sess. House. Doc. no. 1349)   Serial 7102

—— —— National parks portfolio. Department of the interior. [New York, C. Scribner's sons, 1916] 9 p.

nine illustrated pamphlets with 4 pages of introductory text, in portfolio, describing the various national parks.

—— —— Procedure in matters relating to the national parks and the Hot Springs reservation. [Washington, Govt. print. off., 1911] 3 p.

—— —— Progress in the development of the national parks, by Stephen T. Mather, assistant to the Secretary of the interior. Washington, Govt. print. off., 1916. 39 p. incl. illus. (map) tables.

───── ───── Regulations governing rangers in the national park. Washington, Govt. print. off., 1915. 3 p.

───── ───── Report of the general superintendent and landscape engineer of national parks to the Secretary of the interior . . . 1915. Washington, Govt. print. off., 1915. 31 p.

───── ───── Report of the Secretary of the interior . . . Washington, Govt. print. off., 1849─────
Prior to 1907, these reports included information concerning minor parks and national monuments, and summaries of reports on the several parks. Beginning in 1907, only a general review of Park affairs has been included.

───── ───── Rules, regulations and instructions for the information and guidance of officers and enlisted men of the United States army, and of the scouts doing duty in the Yellowstone national park . . . Washington, Govt. print. off., 1907. 35 p.

───── ───── Use of automobiles in national parks. Letter from the acting secretary of the interior, transmitting information in response to Senate resolution of March 9, 1912. [Washington, 1912] 7 p.

───── ───── [Publications relating to individual parks]

───── ───── General information regarding Casa Grande ruin, Arizona . . . [Washington, Govt, print. off., 1913] 31 p. incl. plans.
"This circular is an abstract of a detailed report by J. W. Fewkes, published in the Twenty-eighth annual report of the Bureau of American ethnology." *cf.* p. [1]

───── ───── Proceedings before the secretary of the interior. *In re* applications of A. H. Ward and the Mariposa electrical power company of California for right of way under the regulations prescribed under the act of February 15, 1901 (31 Stats., 790), over government lands in the Yosemite national park. *In re* James D. Phelan, applicant, for rights of way in Hetch Hetchy Valley and Lake Eleanor in the Yosemite national park. Petition for review by the city and county of San Francisco. Washington, Govt. print. off., 1903. 71 p. fold. diagr.

—— —— Report on Sullys Hill park, Casa Grande ruin; the Muir woods, petrified forest, and other national monuments, including list of bird reserves. 1915. Washington, Govt. print. off., 1915. 65 p.

—— —— Report on Wind Cave, Crater Lake, Sullys Hill. Platt, and Mesa Verde national parks and Casa Grande ruin. 1907. Washington, Govt. print. off., 1908. 12 p.

—— —— Report on Wind Cave, Crater Lake, Sullys Hill, and Platt national parks, Casa Grande ruin and Minnesota national forest reserve. 1908. Washington, Govt. print. off., 1909. 20 p. 2 pl.

—— —— Rules and regulations for the government of all bath houses receiving hot water from the United States reservation at Hot Springs, Ark. . . . December 14, 1909. [Washington, Govt. print. off., 1909] 4 p.

—— *Engineer dept.* Reports of the Chief of engineers, U. S. army . . . Washington, Govt. print. off., 19—

[These contain reports of officers in charge of road work in parks]

—— *Forest service.* Annual report of the Forester. Washington, Govt. print. off., 1888——

Information concerning coöperation in park service.

—— —— National forests and national parks. United States, Alaska, and Porto Rico. [map, with insets] 1907. 17.5 x 28.5, 5 x 6.8, 2.1 x 4.7 in.

—— *General land office.* Report of the Commissioner, 1848– Washington, Govt. print. off., 1849–

[Includes information concerning surveys and disposition of public lands out of which national parks and monuments are reserved]

—— *Geological survey.* Folios of the geologic atlas of the United States.

Folios have been published of the Yellowstone national park, Lassen peak, and others.

—— —— Water analyses from the laboratory of the United States Geological survey . . . Washington, Govt. print. off., 1914. 40 p. (Water supply paper 364) Published also as House document 1082, 63d Congress, 2d session.

[Gives analyses of waters of mineral springs in various parts of the country, including Yellowstone national park]

—— *Judge-advocate-general's dept.* (*Army*) United States military reservations, national cemeteries, and military parks. Title, jurisdiction, etc. . . . Rev. ed.: 1916. Washington, Govt. print. off., 1916. 544 p. (War dept. doc. no. 496)

—— *Laws, statutes, etc.* [Laws and regulations] An act to establish a National park service, and for other purposes. Approved Aug. 25, 1916. (Stat. L. ch. 408, p. 535)

—— —— Laws and regulations relating to the Crater Lake national park, Oregon . . . Washington, Govt. print. off., 1908. 13 p.

—— —— Laws, regulations, and general information relating to Glacier national park, Montana. 1910. Washington, Govt. print. off., 1911. 10 p. map.

—— —— Laws and regulations relating to the Hot Springs reservation, Hot Springs, Ark. Washington, Govt. print. off., 1908. 44 p.

—— —— Laws and regulations relating to the Mesa Verde national park, Colorado . . . Washington, Govt. print. off., 1908. 16 p.

—— —— Laws and regulations relating to the Mount Rainier national park, Washington. . . . Washington, Govt. print. off., 1908. 22 p.

—— —— Laws and regulations relating to the Platt national park, Oklahoma . . . Washington, Govt. print. off., 1908. 15 p.

―― ―― Laws and regulations relating to the Sequoia and General Grant national parks, California . . . Washington, Govt. print. off., 1908. 14 p.

―― ―― Laws and regulations relating to the Wind Cave national park, South Dakota . . . Washington, Govt. print. off., 1908. 14 p.

―― ―― Laws and regulations relating to the Yellowstone national park, Wyoming . . . Washington, Govt. print. off., 1908. 22 p.

―― ―― Laws and regulations relating to the Yosemite national park, California. . . . Washington, Govt. print. off., 1908. 23 p.

―― *National park service.* Report of the director of the National park service to the Secretary of the interior, 1917– Washington, Govt. print. off., 1917–

―― ―― General information regarding Casa Grande national monument, Arizona. Washington, Govt. print. off., 1919. 31 p.

―― ―― General information regarding Crater Lake national park, season of 1912-1919. Washington, Govt. print. off., 1912-19. 8 v.
Continued by Rules and regulations, Crater Lake national park, 1920–

―― ―― General information regarding Glacier national park. Season of 1912-1919. Washington, Govt. print. off., 1912-19. 8 v.
Continued by Rules and regulations Glacier national park, 1920–

―― ―― General information regarding the Hot Springs of Arkansas. Washington, Govt. print. off., 1919 14 p.
Continued by Rules and regulations governing Hot Springs reservation, 1919–

―― ―― General information regarding Mesa Verde national park, season of 1912-1919. Washington, Govt. print. off., 1912-19. 8 v.

BIBLIOGRAPHY

Continued by Rules and regulations Mesa Verde national park, 1920–

———— ———— General information regarding Mount Rainier national park. Season of 1912-1919. Washington, Govt. print. off., 1912-19. 8 v.
Continued by Rules and regulations Mount Rainier national park, 1920–

———— ———— General information regarding Sequoia and General Grant national parks. Season of 1912-1919. Washington, Govt. print. off., 1912-19. 8 v.
Continued by Rules and regulations Sequoia and General Grant national parks, 1920–

———— ———— General information regarding Wind Cave national park. Season of 1915-1919. Washington, Govt. print. off., 1915-19. 5 v.
Continued by Rules and regulations, Wind Cave national park, 1920–

———— ———— General information regarding Yellowstone national park. Season of 1912-1919. Washington, Govt. print. off., 1912-19. 8 v.
Continued by Rules and regulations Yellowstone national park, 1920–

———— ———— General information regarding Yosemite national park. Season of 1912-1919. Washington, Govt. print. off., 1912-19. 8 v.
Continued by Rules and regulations Yosemite national park, 1920–

———— ———— General information regarding Rocky Mountain national park. Season of 1916-1919. Washington, Govt. print. off., 1916-19. 4 v.
Continued by Rules and regulations, Rocky Mountain national park, 1920–

———— ———— General information regarding the national monuments, set aside under the act of Congress approved June 8, 1906. Washington, Govt. print. off. 1917. 80 p.

―― ―― The national parks portfolio. [3d ed.] Washington, Govt. print. off., 1921. 266 p.

―― ―― Report on the proposed Sand Dunes national park, Indiana. Washington, Govt. print. off., 1917. 113 p.

[Appendices include hearings on the project held at Chicago, Oct. 30, 1916, miscellaneous letters, resolutions and other documents]

―― ―― Report on Platt and Wind Cave national parks, Sullys Hill park, Casa Grande ruin, Muir Woods, Petrified Forest, and other national monuments, including list of bird reserves. 1911– . . . Washington, Govt. print. off., 1912–

―― ―― Rules and regulations, Grand Canyon national park, 1920– Washington, Govt. print. off., 1920–

―― ―― Rules and regulations, Lafayette national park, 1921– Washington, Govt. print. off., 1921–

―― ―― Statement of appropriations 1879-1918, inclusive, for national parks and national monuments under the jurisdiction of the Secretary of the interior. Comp . . . by Mae A. Schnurr. Washington, Govt. print. off., 1917. 20 p.

―― *Office of public roads.* Report of the director. Washington, Govt. print. off., 1897–

[Information regarding road surveys in national parks]

―― *Superintendent of Crater Lake national park.* Report. 1903-1906, 1910-1915. Washington, Govt. print off., 1903-1915. 10 v.

Reports for 1907–1909 are included in the Report[s] on Wind Cave, Crater Lake, Sullys Hill, Platt and Mesa Verde national parks . . . 1907-1909.

[During 1916 the administration of the national parks was assigned to the Superintendent of national parks, who in his report to the Secretary of the Interior for 1916, included excerpts from the reports of officers in charge of national parks. In April, 1917, the United States national park service was organized and since 1917 full reports of officers in charge of national parks will be found in the reports of the national park service]

―― *Superintendent of Glacier national park.* Report . . . 1911-1915. Washington, Govt. print. off., 1911-15. 5 v.

BIBLIOGRAPHY 157

—— *Superintendent of Hot Springs reservation.* Report
... 1877-1915. Washington, Govt. print. off., 1877-1915.
26 v.

—— *Superintendent of Mesa Verde national park.* Report.
1908-1915. Washington, Govt. print. off., 1908-15. 8 v.

—— *Superintendent of Mount Rainier national park.* Report. 1909/10-1915. Washington, Govt. print. off., 1910-15. 6 v.

—— *Superintendent of national parks.* Annual report. *See* U. S. Dept. of the interior. Annual report of the Superintendent of national parks ... 1916.

—— *Superintendent of Platt national park.* Report. 1913-1915. Washington, Govt. print. off., 1914-15-3 v.

Earlier reports concerning this park were made by the Dept. of the interior. (Before 1906 the park was called Sulphur Springs reservation)

—— *Superintendent of Sequoia and Gen. Grant national parks.* Report ... 1892-1915. Washington Govt. print. off., 1892-15.

—— *Superintendent of Wind Cave national park.* Report. 1913/14— Washington, Govt. print. off., 1914-15.

—— *Superintendent of Yellowstone national park.* Report. ... 1872-1915. Washington, Govt. print. off., 1873-15. 39 v.

For reports of 1873-1874 see Annual report of Secretary of the interior. Apparently no reports were printed in 1875 and 1884.

—— *Superintendent of Yosemite national park.* Report ... 1891-1915. Washington, Govt. print. off., 1899-15. 23 v.

—— *War dept.* New roads in Yellowstone national park. Letter from the acting Secretary of war, transmitting information, in response to Senate resolution of April 2, 1912, relative to the cost of constructing new roads in the Yellowstone national park. ... Washington, Govt. print. off., 1912. 27 p.

―― ―― Regulations for the national military parks and the statutes under which they were organized and are administered. 1914. Washington, Govt. print. off., 1914. 41 p.

―― ―― Stationing of troops of the regular army in national parks. Letter transmitting copy of a letter from ex-secretary Garrison in regard to stationing troops of the regular army in national parks. June 4, 1917. Washington, Govt. print off., 1917. 5 p. (65th Cong., 1st sess. House. Doc. 174)   Serial 7300

―― *Yosemite park commission.* Report of Yosemite park commission. Letter from the Secretary of the interior, transmitting the report of the Yosemite park commission appointed to ascertain what portions of said park are not necessary for park purposes, and also at what place a substantial road can be built from the boundary of said park to the Yosemite Valley grant, together with maps, etc. . . . [Washington, Govt. print. off., 1904] 51 p. plates, fold. maps, fold. tab. (58th Cong., 3d sess. Senate. Doc. 34)   Serial 4764

Yard, Robert S. Glimpses of our national parks 3d ed. . . . Washington, Govt. print. off., 1920. 72 p. illus. (incl. map)

Unofficial Publications: Books and Pamphlets

Allen, Edward F. *ed.* A guide to the national parks of America . . . Rev. ed. New York, McBride, Nast & Company, 1918. 338 p.

American civic association. *Dept. of national and state parks.* National parks: President Taft on a national parks bureau, address to the American civic association. National parks—the need of the future, address by Ambassador Bryce. The need for a bureau of national parks, addresses by Hon. Walter L. Fisher . . . Are national parks worth while? Address by Mr. J. Horace McFarland . . . Washington, D. C., Dept. of national and state parks, American civic association [1912] 30 [2] p. (American civic association.

BIBLIOGRAPHY 159

[Pamphlets] series II, no. 6, Dec. 1912)
Includes addresses on the subject delivered at the 1911 and 1912 conventions of the American civic association.

Branson, Isaac R. Yosemite against corporation greed; shall half of Yosemite national park be destroyed by San Francisco? A thesis against it, by I. R. Branson. Ex-Secretary of the interior Garfield's decision review . . . Aurora, Neb., I. R. Branson, 1909. [30] p.

Bryce, James Bryce, *viscount*. National parks—the need of the future. (In *his* University and historical addresses). New York, 1913. p. 391–406.

[Praises the national park system, advises against the use of automobiles in national parks, and recommends creation of additional parks]

Chittenden, Hiram M. The Yellowstone national park, historical and descriptive. New enl. ed. Cincinnati, Stewart, 1915. 350 p.

[Contains chapters on discovery and later explorations, the national park idea, administrative history of the park, etc.]

Gauss, H. C. National parks. (In *his* American government. New York, 1908. p. 693–705)

Gleason, H. W. National parks and monuments. Address . . . Jan. 3, 1917. Washington, Govt. print. off., 1917. 11 p.

Hall, Ansel F. *ed.* Handbook of Yosemite national park. New York, Putnam, 1921. 347 p.

Mills, Enos A. Your national parks . . . with information to tourists, by Laurence F. Schmeckebier. Boston, Houghton Mifflin company, 1917. 531 p.

Muir, John. Our national parks. New and enl. ed., fully illustrated. Boston and New York, Houghton Mifflin company, 1909. 382 p.

Palmer, T. S. National monuments as wild-life sanctuaries. Address . . . Jan. 4, 1917. Washington, Govt. print. off., 1917. 20 p.

Senn, Nicholas. Our national recreation parks ... With fifty illustrations. Chicago, W. B. Conkey company, 1904. 3 p. l., 11-147 p.

Yard, Robert S. The book of the national parks. New York, Scribner, 1913. 420 p.

Periodical Articles

Beauty of use: water power resources essential to Pacific states limited by proposed enlargement of national parks. Electrical world, Dec. 18, 1920, v. 76: 1201-3.

Bryce, James Bryce, *viscount*. National parks—the need of the future. Outlook, Dec. 14, 1912, v. 102: 811-5.

[Commends the management of some of our national parks, and recommends creation of additional parks]

Chamberlain, A. Scenery as a national asset. Outlook, May 28, 1910, v. 95: 157-69.

[Urges that the government use the national parks as a money-producing asset as Switzerland does]

Claudy, C. H. Our national parks, playgrounds for the people unsurpassed in the world. Scientific American supplement, Nov. 11, 1916, v. 82: 312-13.

[Reports the passage of the National parks service bill and emphasizes the need for such a service in caring for our parks. Includes tabular statements concerning the national parks and monuments, administered by the Interior, Agricultural and War departments]

Controversy over use of water of national parks. Engineering news, May 5, 1921, v. 86: 777-8.

Curtis, W. E. Our national parks and reservations. American academy of political and social science. Annals, March, 1910, v. 35: 231-40.

[Reserves described are of national forests, national parks, national game preserves, national monuments and small game preserves.]

Cutler, J. E. Nation's playgrounds. Suburban life, June, 1913, v. 16: 445-6.

[Descriptive article concerning the national parks]

Dean, W. H. Advertising America. Outing, Aug., 1916, v. 68: 461-9.

["Uncle Sam telling his people about their national parks in language they can understand." Account of the work of Stephen T. Mather, assistant secretary of the interior, in giving publicity to America's great playgrounds. Description of the descriptive booklets and portofolios of the national parks]

—— Our national parks— a seven reel feature [photographs by Herford T. Cowling] Sunset, June, 1916, v. 36: 19-23, 69-70.

[How the photographs and moving picture films are secured by Mr. Cowling for use in the "See America first" campaign, inaugurated by Stephen T. Mather, assistant secretary of the interior]

De Boer, S. R. Landscape architecture in our national forests and parks. American forestry, Nov. 1919, v. 25: 1459-64.

Debt to the people [need of larger appropriations for National park service] Saturday evening post, Jan. 31, 1920, v. 192: 28-29.

Eldridge, M. O. Touring Yellowstone park on government highways. World to-day, Nov. 1910, v. 19: 1263-72.

There are 416 miles of government roads in the Yellowstone Park and adjacent national forests; and 150 miles of horseback trails for use of tourists and for troops and scouts who patrol the park. How the roads are located and constructed.

Fall, Albert B. Value of our national parks. American forestry, June, 1921, v. 27: 359-70.

Graves, H. S. Crisis in national recreation. American forestry, July, 1920, v. 26: 391-400.

Grinnell, J. and Storer, T. R. Animal life as an asset of national parks. Science, Sept. 15, 1916, n. s. v. 44: 375-80.

Johnson, R. U. Dismembering your national park. Outlook, Jan. 30, 1909, v. 91: 252-3.

> [Protest against giving water privileges within the Yosemite to San Francisco]

Koch, F. J. Protecting national parks against poachers. Overland monthly, Feb. 1915, n. s. v. 65: 117-22.

> [Descriptive of the work of Uncle Sam's poacher-catchers in the Yellowstone Park, a garrison of 400 men for service in summer and winter]

Lazenby, Mary E. Luring the people to their playgrounds; what the government is doing to introduce the glories of the national park system to its owners. The Nation's business, June, 1917, v. 5: 37-9.

> [The work of the National park service, and its superintendents, list of publications of the service, and prices of those for sale.]

Lane, Franklin K. National parks as an asset. American forestry, Jan., 1916, v. 22: 22-3.

Lewis, H. H. Managing a national park. Outlook, Aug. 29, 1903, v. 74: 1036-40.

> [Tells how the Yellowstone park is administered by the government]

Lockwood, J. A. Uncle Sam's troopers in National parks of California. Overland monthly, April, 1889, 2d ser., v. 33: 356-68.

> [Objects in sending troops to the national parks are to preserve the timber and vegetation, and protect game and fish]

Mather, S. T. Do you want to lose your parks? A message from the United States government to the American people. Independent, Nov. 13, 1920, v. 104: 220-21.

—— National parks on a business basis. American Review of reviews, April, 1915, v. 51: 429-31.

> [An instructive letter from the new Director of national parks regarding their management for the public welfare]

Mills, Enos A. Exploiting our national parks. New republic, Nov. 10, 1920, v. 24: 272.

Muir, J. Endangering valleys: the Hetch Hetchy valley. Century, Jan., 1909, v. 77: 464-9.

> [Editor believes that an unfortunate precedent has been established in the diversion of a large part of the Yosemite national park from the use of the whole public to the service of a city]

National park amendments to water power bill introduced in Congress. Electrical world, Dec. 11, 1920, v. 76: 1181.

National park improvements. Nation (N. Y.) Feb. 1, 1919, v. 108: 157.

National park service. Independent, May 29, 1916, v. 86: 321.

National park service. Outlook, Feb. 3, 1912, v. 100: 246.

> [Favors establishment of a National park service.]

National parks: a conference. Outlook, Sept. 30, 1911, v. 99: 255-6.

> [Report of National park conference in the Yellowstone, at which the necessity for creation of a Federal park bureau was conceded]

National parks of the United States. Bulletin of the Pan-American union, Sept., 1916, v. 43: 372-86.

> [Description of the parks, well illustrated]

National parks versus National forests. American forestry, Jan. 1917, v. 23: 48-49.

New national parks and their administration. American forestry, June, 1916, v. 22: 366.

Nolen, John. Parks and recreation facilities of the United States. American academy of political and social science. Annals, March, 1910, v. 35: 218-20.

> [Calls attention to the need for a better balanced system of national parks—for creation of parks in the East and other sections of the country as well as in the West]

Our national parks in great danger [provision in water-power bill . . . to grant water-power concessions in national parks] Bird lore, Jan-Feb., 1921, v. 23: 64-65.

Our new national parks. World's work, July, 1920, v. 40: 281-88.

Preparedness and the national park. Country life, June, 1916, v. 30: 48-9.

[A plea for the creation of a national park service to aid in meeting needs of tourists who will visit our national parks while the "War of the nations" makes European travel impossible]

Protecting the tourists in the national parks. Outlook, June, 28, 1916, v. 113: 450-1.

[Reference to hold-ups in Yellowstone park and need of guarding tourists more efficiently. The government forbids tourists in national parks from carrying firearms for self protection]

Report on the national parks situation [as affected by the Water power act] *editorial.* Bird lore, March, 1921, v. 23: 111-13.

Rhoda, Jean. Uncle Sam in the Yosemite. Overland, June, 1913, n. s. v. 61: 590-4.

[During the months from May to November, two troops of U. S. cavalry protect the Yosemite from fires, and enforce restrictions regarding hunting and fishing, etc.]

Saving the Yosemite park. Outlook, Jan. 30, 1909, v. 91: 234-6.

[Protest against using the Hetch Hetchy valley by San Francisco]

Schmeckebier, L. F. National parks from the scientific and educational side. Popular science monthly, June, 1912, v. 80: 530-47.

[Attention is called to publications and maps issued by the scientific bureaus of the government and various learned societies regarding the parks. The contemplated issue by the Department of the interior of short publications describing the phenomena in the various parks and forces that have produced them. An instructive, well illustrated article, in which a bureau of national parks is recommended]

—— Our national parks. National geographic magazine, June, 1912, v. 23: 531-79.

  [A beautifully illustrated article on the different national parks]

Smith, G. O. Nation's playgrounds. American review of reviews, July, 1909, v. 40: 44-8.

  The Director of the Geological survey urges creation of additional mountain parks, which John Muir has termed "fountains of life."

Taylor, G. R. Washington at work: the nation's playgrounds. (illus.) Survey, Jan. 1, 1916, v. 35: 390-3.

  [Some account of the national parks, their administration under the Department of the Interior and a plea for the creation of a national parks bureau]

Trench, J. D. W. The forest and the army. Garden and forests, Feb. 22, 1893, v. 6: 95.

  [If the care of the forests in the national parks and reservations is to be assigned to a portion of the Army, the author believes the War department should include a study of forest conditions in its larger scope of instruction]

United States will capitalize its scenery. Engineering record, Nov. 6, 1915, v. 72: 568-70.

  ["Newly adopted policy of opening up our national parks in the West should bring the country $50,000,000 annually."]

Vestal, A. G. Recreation engineering in our national forests. Illustrated world, Sept., 1921, v. 36: 77-78.

Wanted, a national park service. Outlook, Mar. 1, 1916, v. 112: 491.

Waugh, Frank A. Landscape architecture in the forests. American forestry, March, 1921, v. 27: 142-6.

—— A national park policy. Scientific monthly, April, 1918, v. 6: 305-18.

—— Technical problems in national park development. Scientific monthly, June, 1918, v. 6: 560-67.

Yard, R. S. Director of the nation's playgrounds, what a

practical enthusiast is doing to make our national parks known to the people. Sunset, Sept., 1916, v. 37:27.

[The work of Stephen T. Mather, Secretary Lane's Assistant in executive charge of national parks]

—— National parks peril. Nation (N. Y.) Aug. 21, 1920, v. 111: 208-9.

INDEX

Accounts, 61.
Act for Preservation of American Antiquities, movement for enactment of, 7; scope of, broadened, 7-8; gist of, 17; text of, 84.
Activities of Service subordinate to park preservation, 15; assumption of complete control over, 25-26; descriptive sketch of, 50-59 classification of, 76-77.
Act of Dedication of Yellowstone, outstanding features, 4.
Administration, an anomaly in, 26; Park Service, 60 Yellowstone, 64.
American Automobile Association, 28.
American Civic Association, work of, 11; bulletin, 12.
Animal industry, Bureau of, coöperation with, 54.
Antelope, in Wind Cave Park, 36.
Appropriations, for general superintendent, etc., 10; transferance of, 26; War Department, for parks, 26-27, 32; committee on, visits parks, 27; Interior Dept., for Yellowstone, 32; Agricultural Dept., for Sullys Hill, 37; for Hawaii, limitation on, 39; for Rocky Mountain, do, 39; limitation on expenditure of, in Grand Canyon, 41; for monuments, 43; for fire-fighting emergencies, 52; for maintenance, 57; indirect, for Service at Large, 61-62; for 1922, text of act, 90-93.
Archæology, proposed school of, in Mesa Verde, 38.
Army, U. S., use of in parks, 25-27, 31-32, 34.
Army and Navy Hospital, Hot Springs, 43.
Assistant Director, 60.
Automobile, fees, 17; revenues from, 28; controversy, 28.

Ballinger, Secretary, favors creation of park bureau, 11.
Biological Survey, Bureau of, management of game preserves by, 36, 37, 54.
Birds, protection of, 54.
Boone National Forest, 24.
Bright Angel Trail, 40-41.
Bryce Canyon, Utah, proposed park in, 14.
Buffalo, Yellowstone, 23, 32; Wind Cave, 36; Platt, 37; winter feeding of, 53; vaccination of, 54.

California, cession of park jurisdiction by, 13; use of army in parks of, 26-27; recession of Yosemite by, 34.
Camps, concessioners', 17; free sites for, equipment of with sanitary facilities, etc., 17, 55-56.
"Canadian Argument," the, 11.
Canadian Park Service, 18, 38.
Casa Grande, change in status of, 6 n., 13-14.
Chickasaw Indians, 36.

INDEX

Chief Clerk, 60-61.
Chief of Engineers, U. S. A., park road construction directed by, 26.
Chittenden, General Hiram M., quoted, 4-5.
Choctaw Indians, 36.
Civil Engineering Section, work of, 55, 61.
Cliff Dwellings, 7, 51.
Coconino County, Arizona, toll negotiations with, 40-41.
Colorado, creation of game preserve in, 23.
Colter, John, discovers Yellowstone, 2.
Communication Section, Yellowstone, 65.
Concessions, must produce revenue, 17; highest bidder obtains, in Grand Canyon, 40; general policy regarding, 56.
Congress, civilian control opposed by, 27; Hawaii Park created by, 39.
Conservation of wild life, 53-55.
Coöperation, necessity for emphasized, 18.
Corps of Engineers, U. S. A., Yellowstone exploration of, 3; withdrawal from parks of, 25-26; in Yellowstone, 31; in Crater Lake, 36.
Crater Lake National Park, history, 36; laws, 108-109.

Devils Lake, 37.
Devils Tower, distinction of, as first monument, 8; invulnerability of, 44.
Director, functions of, 60.
Division of Publications, telling work of, 12.
Doane, Lieutenant G. C. See Washburn-Doane expedition.

Editorial Section, 62.

Education facilities, furtherance of, in parks, 17.
Elk, various park herds of, 23, 36, 37: Olympic variety of, 48; winter feeding of, in Yellowstone, 53.
Engineering Section, Yellowstone, 66.
Entomology, Bureau of, coöperation with, 53.

Fall, Secretary, letter of, 22.
Federal Power Commission, restriction on appropriation for, 20; refusal of, to grant licenses in parks, 20-21.
Federal Water Power Act, parks menaced by original, 20; partial repeal of, 20.
Fisher, Secretary, advocates park bureau, 11.
Fisheries, Bureau of, coöperation with, 54-55.
Fishing, regulation of, 54.
Field Service, 61.
Field Service at Large, 61-62.
Forester, Chief, 24, 33.
Forests, protection of, 52-53.
Forest Service, coöperation with, 19, 40, 52.
Folsom, David E., 2.
Fort Yellowstone, 25, 32.

Game preserves, need for, 22-23; recent legislation on 23-24, 36; in Platt, Wind Cave, and Sully's Hill Parks, 36-37; Mount McKinley, 40; Yellowstone, 53; Jacksons Hole, 54.
Garrison, Secretary, letter of, 27.
General Grant National Park, history, 34-35; laws, 106-107. See also Sequoia.
General Superintendent and Landscape Engineer, 9-10.
Geological Survey, Yellowstone

INDEX

explorations of, 3; coöperation with, 53, 58, 64.
Gifts to parks, general authorization for acceptance of, 24.
Glacier National Park, homesteaders' rights in, 38; history, 38-39; laws, 113-116.
Government Free Bath House, 43.
Grand Canyon National Monument, 40.
Grand Canyon National Park, leases in, 12-13; history, 40; laws, 120-121.
Grand Canyon Park Act, unusual provisions of, 40.
Grandfather Mountain, 24.
Grant, President, Act of Dedication signed by, 4.
Grazing, regulation of, 15, 33, 52.
"Great American Spa," the, 42.
Great Northern Railway, activities of, in Glacier Park. 38, 56.

Hawaii National Park, history, 39; laws, 118.
Hayden, Dr. F. V., urges creation of Yellowstone, 4.
Hedges, Cornelius, originator of "National Park Idea," 3.
Hetch Hetchy Valley, 10, 19, 34.
Hitchcock, Secretary, 7.
Homesteaders, rights of, in parks, 38.
Hospital facilities, 57-58.
"Hot Springs Cases," 42 n.
Hot Springs Mountain, 42-43.
Hot Springs National Park, creation, 6; unique nature of, 42; history, 42-43; laws. 122-130.
Hot Springs Reservation, setting aside of, 5; confusion regarding status of, 5-6; exception regarding revenues, 28.
Hunting, prohibition of, 17, 53;

Mount McKinley an exception, 53 n.

Idaho, curious law enacted in, 22-23.
Information Section, Yellowstone, 64.
Inscription Rock, protection of, 51.
Irrigation and power projects, park land hunger of, 21-23.
Irrigation and Reclamation, Senate committee on, 22.

Jacksons Hole, 14, 54.
Jurisdiction, federal, desirability of, 16; present extent of, 25; acquisition of, in California. 25, 34; all of Yellowstone not under, 33; acquisition of in Oregon and Washington, 36; in Oklahoma, 37; in Montana, 38; in Arkansas, 43; makes for order, 57.

Lafayette National Park, history, 41; laws, 121.
Landscape, improvements must harmonize with, 16.
Landscape Engineer, 53, 56.
Landscape Engineering Section, 55-56, 61.
Lane, Secretary, 9, 11, 27, 62.
Langford Hon. N. P., 2-3, 31.
Lassen Volcanic National Park, history, 39-40; laws, 118-119.
Law Section, 62-63.
Lewis and Clarke, skirting of Yellowstone region by, 2.
Light and Power Section, Yellowstone, 65.

Machinery Section, Yellowstone, 65-66.
Mackinac Island, former park on, 44.
Maintenance, 57.

Mammoth Cave, proposed park to include, 14.
Mariposa Grove, 33.
Medical Service, 57-58.
Mesa Verde National Park, permits to excavate in, 37; history, 37-38; ruins in, 51; laws, 112-113.
Mining claims, acquisition of in Greater Yellowstone area permissible, 14; Supreme Court decision regarding, 24-25; further location forbidden in Mount Rainier, 35; discretionary allowance of in Grand Canyon, 40; no restrictions on in Mount McKinley, 40.
Montezuma County, Colorado, 37.
Motion pictures, 58-59.
Motor vehicles, 17.
Mount Desert Island, 41.
Mount Lassen, 39.
Mount McKinley National Park, history, 40; laws, 119-120.
Mount Rainier National Park, U. S. Engineers in, 26, 35; history, 35-36; hotel system in, 56; laws, 107-108.
Mount Whitney, Greater Sequoia area includes, 14.
Muir, John, opposes Hetch Hetchy project, 10.
Muir Woods, 44.
Mukuntuweap National Monument, 41.
Museums, establishment of directed, 17; Mesa Verde, 38.

National Geographic Society, gifts of, 24, 35.
National Monuments, power of President to create, 7; distinction between parks and, 8; factor determining administration of, 44; under Dept. of Interior, 43-46; under War Department, 47; under Dept. of Agriculture, 48.
National park, the first, 5-7.
National park conferences, 9, 11.
"National Park Idea," the, origin of, 2-3; gist, 19; menaced, 19-20; versus the automobile, 28; determines Service's activities, 50.
National Park Service Act, amendments to, 12-13; text of, 87-88.
National park system, beginning of, 1, 4; oldest member of, 5; result of the "National Park Idea," 7; prior to 1916, 8-9.
National Park-to-Park-Highway, 27-28.
National parks, projects for additional, 14, 18-19, 24; list of, 29-30; individual sketches of, 31-43; growth of interest in, 49.
National parks portfolio, 12.

Oklahoma, constitutional provision of regarding federal jurisdiction, 37.

Painting Section, Yellowstone, 65.
Patents and Miscellaneous, Division, 9.
Payne, Secretary, opposition of, to park exploitation, 21-22.
Personnel, 61.
Petrified Forest, 44.
Platt National Park, history, 36-37; laws, 110-111.
Poaching, 32, 40, 53.
Post Office Department, parcel post deliveries by, in Yosemite, 57.
President of the United States, the, discretionary power of, to create monuments, 7; rules for

INDEX

Hot Springs hospital to be made by, 43.
Private holdings, objections to, 16; elimination of, in Sequoia, 24, 35; in Wind Cave, 36; exchange of timber authorized for, in Glacier, 39.
Privileges, leasing of, 15.
"Profitable Speculation," a, 3.
Prospecting, Secretary may allow, in Grand Canyon, 40.
Protection service, general, 57; Yellowstone, 64.
Publications, 62, 78-79.
Publications Section, 63.
Publicity, 58, 78-79.
Public Health Service, 56, 58.
Public lands committees, hearings before, 12.

Railroad Administration, 18.
Rangers, civilian force of created, 27; soldiers used as, 32; in Mount Rainier, 35.
Recreation, encouragement of, in parks, 17.
Revenues, expenditures from, 10; must not impose burden, 17; sources of, 31; comparison of, with appropriations, 28; change in disposition of, 28; provision regarding in Yosemite, 34.
Roads and trails, work on, by U. S. Engineer Corps, 25-26; maintenance of, 57.
Rocky Mountain National Park, history, 39; laws, 116-118.
Roosevelt, President, 14.

San Francisco, water supply for, 10.
Sand Dunes, Lake Michigan, proposed park including, 14.
Sanitation, 57, 65.
Scientific bureaus, coöperation with, enjoined, 17-18.
Secretary of Agriculture, coöperation of, in making monument rules and regulations, 7.
Secretary of the Interior, to control Yellowstone, 4; Hot Springs administered by, 5-6; monument regulations made by, 7; office of, reorganized, 9; alluded to, 13, 26, 32.
Secretary of War, monument rules and regulations to be made by, 7; alluded to, 26, 32.
Sequoia National Park, proposed enlargement of, 14, 19; elimination of private holdings in, 24, 35; history, 34-35; laws, 104-106.
Sieur de Monts National Monument, 41.
Smithsonian Institution, archæological researches of, in Mesa Verde, 38; coöperation with, 52.
Standards, Bureau of coöperation with, 51.
Sullys Hill National Park, history, 37; laws, 111-112.
Sulphur, Oklahoma, 37.
Sulphur Springs Reservation, 36.

Taft, President, urges establishment of parks bureau, 12; on Casa Grande, 13 n.; vetoes Mesa Verde amendment, 37.
Taft, Secretary, 7.
Three Tetons, the, 14, 19.
Timber, restrictions on cutting of, 16, 53; exchanges of, authorized, 39.
Toll roads, 41.
Transportation Section, Yellowstone, 65.
Tumacacori Mission, restoration of, 51.

United States Commissioners, 25, 32, 38, 43, 57.

United States Marshals, 33.

Vandals, 44, 51.

War Department, Washburn-Doane escort furnished by, 3; relinquishment of park protection by, 25-26.
Washburn, General Henry D. See Washburn-Doane Expedition.
Washburn-Doane Expedition, 3, 4, 31.
Water power, utilization of, in parks, 53, 56.
Waterton Lakes Park, 38.
Weather Bureau, coöperation with, 64.
"Western Monthly," the, 2.
Wilson, President, 13-14.
Wilson, Secretary, 7.
Wind Cave National Park, history, 36; laws, 109-110.

Yellowstone National Park, creation of, 1; first superintendent of, 2; Act of Dedication of, 4; distinction of, as first national park, 4; proposed enlargement of, 14, 19; proposed construction of reservoir in, 21-22; army activities in, 25-26; appropriations for, under War Dept., 26; withdrawal of troops from, 27, 33; civilian administration of, 31, army administration of, 32; history, 31-33; landmark in legislation for, 32; grazing forbidden in, 33; organization, 63; laws, 93-98.
Yellowstone Region, early accounts of derided, 1-2; first expedition to, 2; Washburn-Doane Exploration of, 3; Geological Survey—Engineer Corps exploration of, 3; project for erection of into park, 4.
Yosemite National Park, construction of reservoir in, 10; history, 33-34; army activities in, 34; laws, 98-104.
Yosemite National Park Company, 56.

Zion National Monument, 42.
Zion National Park, history, 41-42; laws, 121.

W-3